Contributing to Family and Community

A unit exploring the many people and the many ways in which members of families and communities help meet one another's needs

Critical Challenges
ACROSS THE CURRICULUM

Authors

Irene Agelatos

Susan Johnson

Jennifer Lewis

Roberta MacQuarrie

Jan Nicol

Brandi Robinson

Elaine Spracklin

May Wong

Lynn Zuehlke

Illustrator

Danna deGroot

Photographer

Alene Petovello

Editors

Mary Abbott

Carole Ford

Roland Case

The Critical
Thinking Cooperative

BRITISH
COLUMBIA

Series published by

The Critical Thinking Cooperative
Richmond School District
7811 Granville Ave.
Richmond, British Columbia V6Y 3E3
tel: 604-668-6069; fax: 604-668-6191
e-mail: mmcdermid@richmond.sd38.bc.ca

Cover design:	Antonio Banyard
Interior design:	M. Kathie Wraight, Field Programs, Simon Fraser University
Production:	Carpe Diem Educational Consulting, Inc.
Cover photograph:	© Vancouver School Board; Josh Benson, photographer, 2002

© *2003 Ministry of Education, Province of British Columbia*

National Library of Canada Cataloguing in Publication Data

Main entry under title:

Contributing to family and community : a unit exploring the many people
and the many ways in which members of families and communities help meet
one another's needs / authors, Irene Agelatos ... [et al.] ;
illustrator, Danna deGroot ; photographer, Alene Petovello ; editors,
Mary Abbott, Carole Ford, Roland Case.

(Critical challenges across the curriculum series, ISSN 1205-9730)
Copublished by: Ministry of Education, British Columbia.
Includes bibliographical references.
ISBN 0-86491-250-1

   1. Community life--Study and teaching (Elementary) 2.
Community--Study and teaching (Elementary) 2. Critical thinking--Study
and teaching (Elementary) I. Case, Roland, 1951- II. Ford, Carole
Lorraine, 1942- III. Abbott, Mary, 1950- IV. Agelatos, Irene. V.
British Columbia. Ministry of Education. VI. Critical Thinking
Cooperative. VII. Series.
LB1584.5.C3C65 2003   372.83'044   C2003-910351-X

Introductions

Critical Challenges

Blackline Masters

Table of Contents

Foreword

Critical Challenges Across the Curriculum is an ongoing series of teacher resources focused on infusing critical thinking into every school subject. Two features distinguish this series from the many other publications that support critical thinking—our *content-embedded* approach and our emphasis on *teaching the intellectual tools.*

Our approach is to embed critical thinking by presenting focused questions or challenges that invite critical student reflection about the content of the curriculum. We do not see critical thinking as a generic set of skills or processes that can be developed independently of content and context. Nor do we believe that critical thinking can be adequately addressed as an add-on to the curriculum. Rather, critical thinking is profitably viewed as a way to teach the content of the curriculum. Teachers can help students understand the subject matter, as opposed to merely recalling it, by providing continuing opportunities for thoughtful analysis of issues that are central to the curriculum.

The second distinguishing feature of this series is its emphasis on systematically teaching a full range of tools for critical thinking. Much of the frustration that teachers experience when inviting students to think critically stems from students' lack of the relevant intellectual tools. No doubt some students will figure things out for themselves, but most of the rest will perform at higher levels only if they are taught the requisite tools for the job. For this reason, every critical challenge is accompanied with a list of the tools needed to respond competently, and considerable attention is paid in the suggested activities to detailing how these tools may be taught and assessed.

The British Columbia Ministry of Education has greatly contributed to our work through grants to Richmond, Delta and Maple Ridge school districts to support the efforts of 23 teams of educators associated with *TC²* partners around the province. Over the past two years, through Networks in Teacher Development in Social Studies projects, teachers at all levels have been creating and piloting materials in social studies using a critical thinking approach. The upshot of their efforts is a substantial collection of teacher-developed resources that involve students in thinking critically about social studies, and that teach them the tools to do this well.

We are especially pleased that the Ministry, as part of its larger initiative to support social studies in British Columbia, is sponsoring publication of twelve resources in this series—one for each grade level from kindergarten to grade 11.

We join with the Ministry in hoping that teachers will find these resources of use in their ongoing efforts to make social studies a critically thoughtful, engaging and valuable subject.

Roland Case and LeRoi Daniels

Series Editors

Many people have contributed to the project that has made publication of this resource possible. Maureen McDermid deserves enormous credit for coordinating our efforts. We thank Bruce Beairsto (Richmond), Steve Cardwell (Delta) and Lindy Jones (Maple Ridge) for their leadership and Mary Abbott, LeRoi Daniels, Elaine Decker, Patricia Finlay, Karyl Mills and Neil Smith for help in facilitating the project. We appreciate Shelley Hallock's much needed proofreading and Amy Tang's editorial support. The Vancouver Foundation's financial support of this project was both generous and greatly appreciated. And finally we are indebted to the hundreds of educators who contributed their time and efforts to developing and piloting resources, and to the team leaders listed below who supported these dedicated educators over the past two years.

Acknowledgements

	Partner representatives	Team mentors
Abbotsford District #34	Bruce Mills	Karen Saenger Tina Hinds
BC Intermediate Teachers' Association	Paul Wood	Dorothea Hines
BC Primary Teachers' Association	Bonnie Jesten	Carolyn Edwards
BC Social Studies Teachers' Association	Wayne Axford	Violet Columbara
BC Teacher-Librarians' Association	Mark Roberts Joan Eaton	Bonnie McComb
Burnaby District #41	Mat Hassen	Lisa Schultz
Central Okanagan District #23	Mike Roberts	Wally Swarchuk
Coast Mountain District #82	Sharon Beedle	Christine Foster
Delta District #37	Steve Cardwell	Cheryl Norman Sandra Peel
Greater Victoria District #61	Tanis Carlow	Harry Lewis Tim Bradshaw
Malaspina University College	Mike Grant	Neil Smith
Maple Ridge District #42	Lindy Jones	Patti Taunton
Nanaimo District #68	Leona Kyrytow	Mary-Lynn Epps Leona Kyrytow
North Vancouver District #44	Cathy Molinski	Sandra Kinnon
Okanagan Similkameen #53	Jim Insley	Greg Smith Barbra Paterson
Prince Rupert District #52	Leah Robinson	Leah Robinson
Richmond District #38	Betty Eades	Mike Perry-Whittingham Catriona Misfeldt
Saanich District #63	Sheila Miller	Susan McRae
Simon Fraser University	Roland Case	Roland Case
Surrey District #36	Sherri Mohoruk	Alice Tiles
University of British Columbia	Linda Farr Darling	Linda Farr Darling
Vancouver District #39	Frank McCormick	Phyllis Schwartz
West Vancouver District #45 & West Vancouver Teachers' Association	Geoff Jopson	Bronwen Gouws

Guide to Lesson Format

Each **critical challenge** is a **question** or **task** which is the focal activity upon which the lesson is based. An **overview** describes the topic and the main activities that students undertake.

Broad understanding is the intended curricular understanding that will emerge as students work through the challenge.

Requisite tools provide an inventory of specific intellectual resources that students need to competently address the critical challenge:

Background knowledge — the information about the topic required for thoughtful reflection;

Criteria for judgment — the considerations or grounds for deciding which of the alternatives is the most sensible or appropriate;

Critical thinking vocabulary — the concepts and distinctions that help to think critically about the topic;

Thinking strategies — procedures, organizers, models or algorithms that help in thinking through the challenge;

Habits of mind — the values and attitudes of a careful and conscientious thinker that are especially relevant to the critical challenge.

The body of the lesson is found under **suggested activities** which indicate how the critical challenge may be introduced and how the requisite tools may be taught.

Where relevant, **sessions** indicate where each anticipated new lesson would begin and the blackline masters needed for that session.

Down the left-hand panel is a handy **summary of main tasks** or activities for each session.

Icons along the right-hand side point out where specific tools are addressed.

Also provided in **evaluation** are assessment criteria and procedures, and in **extension** are found suggestions for further exploration or broader application of key ideas.

References cited in the suggested activities or recommended for additional information are often listed.

Blackline masters *follow each lesson. These are the reproducible learning resources referred to in the suggested activities. They serve a wide range of purposes:*

- **assessment rubrics** *identify suggested criteria and standards for evaluating student work;*

- **briefing sheets** *provide background information for students;*

- **data charts** *contain various organizers for recording and analysing information;*

- **documents** *refer to primary source material including paintings and other illustrations;*

- **student activities** *provide questions and tasks for students to complete;*

- **transparencies** *refer to material that can be converted to a transparency for use on an overhead projector.*

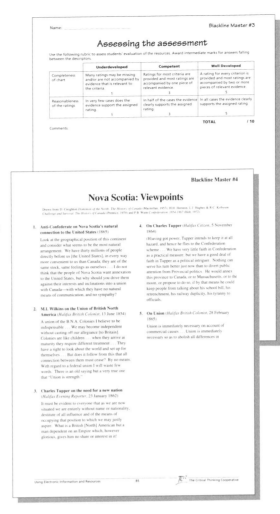

Electronic sourcebook *is a web-based supplement to our print publications. These materials include colour reproductions of pictures, primary documents, and updated links to other sites.*

- *If electronic resources had been developed at the time of publication, the available resources are referenced in the Suggested Activities.*

- *Periodically we update or supplement the print volumes with additional electronic information and resources.*

To locate referenced materials or to see whether new material has been developed, access our website and look for the title of this publication under the Electronic Sourcebook *heading (www.tc2.ca/pub/sourcebook).*

For more information about our model of critical thinking consult our website — www.tc2.ca.

Family roles

1

What we would miss

2 sessions

In this introductory challenge, students are introduced to the many aspects of a community that are important to them. While listening to the story *Alexander, Who's Not (Do you hear me? I mean it!) Going to Move*, students identify the people, places, things and activities that Alexander will miss because his family is moving away. Next, students brainstorm features of their own neighbourhood. After developing criteria for determining importance, students pick three people, places, things and activities that they value. Finally, students select the one aspect from each category that they would miss most if their family had to move away. Students draw pictures of their prized neighbourhood features and give reasons for their choices. These pictures are displayed on a giant wall map of the community.

2

Who is contributing?

2 sessions

This challenge explores the many significant contributions that people make to families and communities. In the book *Wanda's Roses* by Pat Brisson, students identify a range of positive contributions made by characters in the story. Students then sort cards depicting various situations to determine whether or not these people are contributing to others or merely making use of services. Students then consider that some contributions may be more significant than others because of the needs they serve, the number of people affected or the duration of the benefit. Students examine a set of situations and determine how significantly these people are contributing to their families or communities.

3

Contributions in pictures

3 sessions

In this challenge, students learn to extract information from photographs as they extend their understanding of the different community helpers and the contributions each makes. Students take on the role of detective in looking for clues in photographs depicting various community helpers in order to answer the questions: what, where, who and why. They then use their findings to explain how the person depicted in the photograph is contributing to the community.

4

Is this a community?

5 sessions

In this challenge, students learn that a community, in the true sense of the word, is not characterized by the presence of any particular people, places or things, but by a special kind of activity (positive interactions among the members). As an introduction, students observe three role-plays by older students, each illustrating a different theme—no interactions, positive interactions and negative interactions. Students then role-play these different forms of interaction in a typical classroom situation. Based on these experiences, students learn that a community requires interaction among members and the interactions must help people meet their needs. Students are given a number of stories with accompanying drawings about various groups of people. They learn to identify the people, places, things and activities in the scenes and to sort this information according to possible conclusions. After a practice example, students determine which of these group situations represent a community (mutually beneficial interactions) and which do not.

5

Our own community adventure

3 sessions

The focus of this challenge turns more directly to the places and roles within the students' surrounding community. Students begin by identifying the places and community roles represented in a book, *On the Town: A Community Adventure* by Judith Caseley. Students are then given cards identifying many different places. Their job is to decide whether these places are found in their own community. Students play two versions of a game matching these places with the services and people (roles) that they could expect to find at each site. Finally, students write their own community adventure story, accommodating two places and two services identified on cards they have been randomly assigned.

6	**A most important contribution** 5 sessions	In this challenge, students learn about a particular community role or helper. Students gather information from interviews, field trips or picture books, about the contributions made by their allotted role. Based on their research, students select four important contributions and decide which one of these is their role's most important contribution towards meeting the diverse needs of people in the community. Students send a note of appreciation to a representative of their community role, acknowledging his or her help and expressing special thanks for making the most important contribution attached to this role. Students share their information with the rest of the class and draw pictures of various features associated with their role.
7	**Who am I?** 1 session	In this challenge, students reinforce and expand their knowledge of community roles in the course of playing a game of charades. Students are assigned a place in the community and they must prepare a dramatization of a role found in that place. Among other criteria for an effective charade, students must indicate an important need met by their assigned role. Students practice their charade with team members and then perform them before the rest of the class who must guess the role.
8	**A three-star community?** 5 sessions	In this final challenge, students bring closure to their exploration of the ways in which community members help to meet each other's needs. Students assemble evidence of community contributions accumulated throughout the unit in preparation for a "report card" or assessment of their community. Students study the evidence amassed on a giant wall chart, including evidence that community needs may not always be met. Students are introduced to three levels of "community stardom" and assign a rating to their community. As an extension, students create a certificate of merit for their community.

In addition to the materials provided in this volume, the supplementary resources listed below are also recommended. The following symbols identify the role of these resources in completing each critical challenge:

N   **Necessary**   The identified resource is necessary to complete the critical challenge as planned.

O   **Options**   The identified resource or one of the other options identified is necessary to complete the critical challenge as planned.

U   **Useful**   The identified resource is helpful, but not necessary, in completing the critical challenge as planned.

		Title	Description	Bibliographic information
1	N	*Alexander, Who's Not (Do you hear me? I mean it!) Going to Move*	Student picture book	Viorst, Judith. (1998). Aladdin (New York)
2	N	*Wanda's Roses*	Student picture book	Brisson, Pat. (2000). Boyds Mills Press (Honesdale, PA)
5	O	*Franklin's Neighbourhood*	Student picture book	Bourgeois, Paulette. (1999). Kids Can Press (Toronto)
	O	*On The Town: A Community Adventure*	Student picture book	Caseley, Judith. (2002). Harper Collins
6	O	*Franklin's Neighbourhood*	Student picture book	Bourgeois, Paulette. (1999). Kids Can Press (Toronto)
	O	*On The Town: A Community Adventure*	Student picture book	Caseley, Judith. (2002). Harper Collins
	U	A large array of picture books on community places and roles	Student picture books	See References
8	U	*I Can Make a Difference*	Teacher reference	Ford, Carole *et al*. (2003). The Critical Thinking Cooperative and Ministry of Education, British Columbia. (Richmond)

An important goal of the critical challenge approach is to embed critical thinking into the teaching of the curriculum. The chart below identifies which learning outcomes prescribed in the British Columbia Integrated Resource Packages are addressed by each critical challenge. For connections with curriculum documents in other provinces look for the title of this publication on the *TC²* website (www.tc2.ca). The following symbols describe the extent to which each learning outcome is satisfied:

X **Fully met** Completing the critical challenge would fully satisfy the prescribed learning outcome.

/ **Partially met** Completing the critical challenge would partially satisfy the prescribed learning outcome.

Grade 2/3 Outcomes

Code	Emotional and social development	Code	Intellectual development	Code	Social responsibility
1 2 3 4 5 6 7 8 /	Demonstrate a willingness to communicate a range of feelings and ideas (English language arts)	1 2 3 4 6 8 / /	Organize details and information to make simple charts, webs, or illustrations (English Language Arts) / Draw simple interpretations from personal experiences, oral sources, and from visual and written representations (Social Studies) / Collect and record information from a variety of sources and experiences (Social Studies) / Sort, organize, and represent specific information (English Language Arts)	2 3 4 5 6 7 8 X	Describe ways members of a community meet each other's needs (Social Studies)
1 2 4 8 /	Identify an issue and provide several reasons to support a position (Social Studies)	1 2 3 4 5 /	Use picture clues to predict content and make connections between illustrations and written text (English Language Arts)		
2 3 4 /	Identify thoughtful, caring behaviours (personal planning)	1 2 3 4 6 / /	Create a variety of personal communications, including charts, journals, lists, illustrations, and stories (English Language Arts) / Create images based on objects, places, events, or issues in their classroom, school, and community		

What we would miss

Critical Challenge

Critical Question

What person, place, thing and activity would you most miss if your family moved from the neighbourhood?

Overview

In this introductory challenge, students are introduced to the many aspects of a community that are important to them. While listening to the story *Alexander, Who's Not (Do you hear me? I mean it!) Going to Move*, students identify the people, places, things and activities that Alexander will miss because his family is moving away. Next, students brainstorm features of their own neighbourhood. After developing criteria for determining importance, students pick three people, places, things and activities that they value. Finally, students select the one aspect from each category that they would miss most if their family had to move away. Students draw pictures of their prized neighbourhood features and give reasons for their choices. These pictures are displayed on a giant wall map of the community.

Objectives

Broad understanding

Many aspects of a community are important to the people who live there.

Requisite tools

Background knowledge
- knowledge of neighbourhood features

Criteria for judgment
- criteria for important community features (e.g., provide benefit, not likely found in another community, have strong positive attachment)

Critical thinking vocabulary

Thinking strategies
- web

Habits of mind
- attention to detail

Suggested Activities

Preview story

➤ We introduce this challenge with the story *Alexander, Who's Not (Do you hear me? I mean it!) Going to Move*, by Judith Viorst. It tells of a young boy who complains about having to move away because he will miss many valued features of his neighbourhood. If this picture book is not readily available, use another book that focuses on attachment to a neighbourhood. In this challenge, we refer frequently to "neighbourhood" and less so to "community." The distinction we want to explore in later challenges is that a neighbourhood is a "true" community only if the residents have mutually beneficial interactions. In other words, groups of people living in a common location without positive interactions are not considered to be a "true" community.

Develop giant wall map

➤ As part of an ongoing resource to help students locate the important places in their community, we recommend creating a giant wall map of your community, or at least of the surrounding area (including, if possible, sectors where common services—police, library, bakery and so on—are found). To create the map, project an overheard transparency of a published map onto large sheets or rolls of paper attached to a section of the classroom wall (the larger the paper, the better). Orient the map on the wall so that it matches the directions that one would head towards if trying to reach these locations in the community. Initially, trace only the outline of the streets and print their names. Allow space around the map's perimeter for student drawings of important people and things. You may want to paste a Styrofoam block or drawing of the school on its map site. As the unit progresses, students will add their own special places to the map and try to locate places they have visited or studied. You may want to assemble material such as Styrofoam blocks that students could use to mount pictures of these places. The pictures can always be pasted directly on the map, but three-dimensional relief is more effective.

knowledge of unit

Session One — *Blackline Master #1*

Introduce the story

➤ Display a toy moving van or a picture of one. Discuss what it would mean if students saw such a truck parked on their street (people might be moving away or new people arriving). Ask students how they would feel if the moving van was in front of their home. Invite students to share experiences of moving away from a neighbourhood. What is hard about moving? What is good about moving? After students have shared their experiences, explain that you are going to read a story about a boy named Alexander who has strong opinions about moving. Show students the cover of the book *Alexander, Who's Not (Do you hear me? I mean it!) Going to Move*, by Judith Viorst. Read the title blandly and ask students how Alexander might say it. Direct students to look at Alexander's face for clues as to how he might be feeling (e.g., afraid, sad, worried). Invite several students to read the title with feeling.

Read story

web

➤ Before reading the story, instruct students to stop you by raising their hand every time you read something that Alexander will miss because he is moving from his neighbourhood. As students offer suggestions, record these ideas on a chart or chalkboard, clustering their ideas into four groups:

- *people* (e.g., best friend Paul, baby sitter Rachel);

- *places* (e.g., tree house, Rooney's roof, the lot next to Albert's house);

- *things* (e.g., Baldwin's dog, great Halloween treats);

- *activities* (e.g., car pooling, winning the sack race, spitting far, selling lemonade).

Do not label the categories at this point. After the story is finished and many features have been identified, draw a circle around each category. Ask students to look for a common theme in each grouping. Help students see that a neighbourhood is made up of people, places, things (living and inanimate) and activities (what people do). Print each label above the appropriate group of ideas. Print the title "Alexander's neighbourhood" above the labels and draw a circle around it. Create a web by drawing lines from the title to each circled category.

Identify features of students' neighbourhood

knowledge of neighbourhood

attention to detail

➤ Remind students that many aspects of Alexander's neighbourhood were special to him. Invite students to think of the special features of their own neighbourhood. Distribute an enlarged copy (11 x 17) of *Our neighbourhood* (Blackline Master #1) to each pair of students. Ask students to work with their partner to list the special people, places, things and activities in their neighbourhood. After students have developed a preliminary list, take the class outside looking for ideas to add to their lists. If you have created the giant map, locate the school on the map and trace the route that you propose for your field study. While outside, assist students with their observations by pointing out, and by asking students to point out, any notable people, places, things and activities. Encourage students to record each aspect in the proper category on Blackline Master #1 and to have at least two items in each category. Upon your return to the classroom, ask a few students to retrace the route on the map and, if possible, locate a few features that were observed. As an extension, invite students to watch for any additional special features on their way home from school.

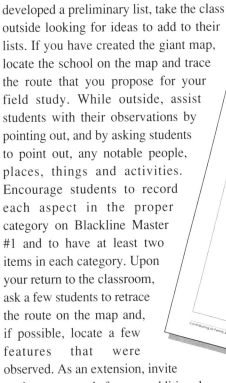

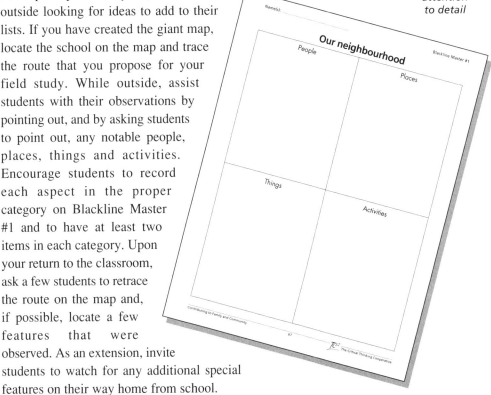

Assemble community web

➤ Refer students to the web of special features in Alexander's neighbourhood. Invite students to create a class web of their own neighbourhood, by transferring the features they recorded on Blackline Master #1 to a large sheet of paper that you will have prepared with labels for the four kinds of features and with a title, "Features of our neighbourhood." Ask students to neatly transcribe their features to slips of paper and paste them underneath the appropriate labels on the large sheet. Alternatively, ask students to record their features directly on the large sheet. You may want to colour code the four kinds of features, either by using coloured paper or coloured pens.

Develop criteria for important community features

➤ Invite students to study the giant web and look for features in each category that they would miss if they had to move away. Ask students to volunteer what they would miss and to explain why. On the board, make a list of the kinds of reasons they offer. After several suggestions and explanations, ask students to look for common factors in the list of reasons. Guide them in identifying three or four criteria for deciding what makes a community feature important or memorable. These might include the following:

important features of a community

- the person has *strong positive feelings* about the feature;
- the feature provides a *benefit to the person*;
- the feature is *not likely to be found in another community.*

Present the critical challenge

➤ Refer students back to the class web of features of the neighbourhood. Invite them to imagine they must move away from the community. What would they miss the most? Distribute a copy of the first sheet of *What I would miss the most* (Blackline Master #2A) to each student. Instruct students to think of three features for each of the four categories. Students should list these features in the appropriate boxes. When they have completed this task, present the critical question:

What person, place, thing and activity would you most miss if your family moved from the neighbourhood?

Students are to decide for each category which one of the three is the most important feature— the feature they would miss most—and offer reasons for their answer. When making their choice and when explaining why, remind students to use the criteria discussed earlier.

➤ When students have completed Blackline Master #2A, distribute a copy of Blackline Master #2B to each student. Students are to draw pictures of the four most prized features for inclusion on the giant map. If students have difficulty drawing within the boxes, enlarge Blackline Master #2B to ledger size (11 x 17). Depending on the size of your giant map, you may afterwards want to reduce their drawings so they will fit the scale of the map. When completed, ask students to cut out their drawings and paste their "Place" pictures (on Styrofoam blocks or directly on the map) in the appropriate location. You will need to help students locate the correct spot on the map. Ask students to explain to the class why they will most miss this place. The "People" and "Things" pictures can be attached along the sides of the map. You may want to paste these pictures yourself and over a few days as you continue with the next challenge, ask students to point out to the class their prized person and thing and to explain their choices. The "Activity" pictures can be handled like the "People" and "Things" pictures, or they could be reduced in size on the photocopier, glued to toothpicks and mounted like flags on the map, attached by small pieces of modeling clay or stuck into a Styrofoam block.

Evaluation

Blackline Master #3

➤ Assess students' understanding of the features of their neighbourhood using the rubric *Assessing community features* (Blackline Master #3). The sources of evidence and the two criteria for this assessment are as follows:

- use students' responses to *Our neighbourhood* (Blackline Master #1) to assess their ability to identify the different features of their neighbourhood;

- use students' responses and reasons for their selection of important features recorded on *What I would miss the most* (Blackline Master #2A) to assess their ability to select important neighbourhood features.

Reaching the "basic understanding" level on the rubric may be appropriate for many primary students who are new to the study of community.

References

Viorst, Judith. (1998). *Alexander, Who's Not (Do you hear me? I mean it!) Going to Move* (illustrated by Robin Preiss Glasser). New York: Aladdin. (ISBN 0-689-31958-4)

Who is contributing?

Critical Challenge

Critical Question

Are the people in this story contributing a lot, some, or a little to their family or community?

Overview

This challenge explores the many significant contributions that people make to families and communities. In the book *Wanda's Roses* by Pat Brisson, students identify a range of positive contributions made by characters in the story. Students then sort cards depicting various situations to determine whether or not these people are contributing to others or merely making use of services. Students then consider that some contributions may be more significant than others because of the needs they serve, the number of people affected or the duration of the benefit. Students examine a set of situations and determine how significantly these people are contributing to their families or communities.

Objectives

Broad understanding

Contributing to family or community is not the same as using the services and facilities provided. In a community, people contribute in many different ways that benefit others.

Requisite tools

Background knowledge
- knowledge of community interactions and their effects

Criteria for judgment
- criteria for significant contribution (e.g., helps many people meet important needs for a long time)

Critical thinking vocabulary
- making a contribution

Thinking strategies
- think of a time
- sorting of cards

Habits of mind

Suggested Activities

think of a time

Share personal helping experiences

➤ Invite the class to think of a time when they helped someone. Without expecting answers, prompt students' thinking with the following questions:

- Who did you help?
- What did you do?
- How did you feel?
- What happened because you helped?
- How did they feel?

Next, invite students to think of a time when someone helped them. Prompt students' thinking with the following questions:

- Who helped you?
- What did they do?
- How did you feel?
- What happened because they helped?
- How did the other person feel?

Now, ask students to choose one of their ideas to share. Quickly go around the room encouraging each student to provide a one-sentence example of helping or being helped (e.g., I helped my grandma weed her garden) and a brief indication of how it felt (e.g., I felt proud).

Introduce the book

➤ Announce that you are about to read a story about people who helped each other. The book is *Wanda's Roses* by Pat Brisson. (It tells the story of a young girl's attempts to cultivate a bush, which she discovers in a junk-filled lot. Because of her persistence in caring for and protecting what she insists is a rosebush, the neighbours plant roses in the lot, fulfilling Wanda's dream of a rose garden fit for a king.) Introduce the book by asking students what the picture on the cover makes them wonder about the story. Point out that the young girl is looking at the leafless bush growing among the garbage in the lot. Invite students to anticipate what this suggests about the story.

Read the story

➤ Before reading the story, explain that there are six characters (they are listed in the chart below). Assign each student a number from one to six, and then attach a number to each character in the story (i.e., Wanda is "one," Mrs. Turner is "two" and so on). Each time one of the characters appears in the story, students with that number are to listen carefully for the things their character does to help other people.

➤ After reading the story, ask each group of students to recall the name of its character and what that person did in the story to help out. Record students' responses in a chart as indicated below. For each helpful action, invite students to indicate the result or effect of the action on the character and on others. Point out that when people help each other, the results are usually positive—people usually feel better and are better off.

*knowledge of
community
interactions*

Helping others

People in the story	What they did to help each other	Result (what happened)
Wanda	• *cared for the bush* • *cleaned up around the bush* • *invited the neighbours for tea* • *tied roses on the bush* • *persisted*	• *Wanda felt excited* • *the lot looked better* • *the neighbours appreciated the difference in appearance*
Mrs. Turner	• *brought a rose bush*	• *Wanda felt happy* • *Mrs. Turner felt happy* • *the lot looked better*
Mr. Claudel	• *helped Wanda clean up*	• *Wanda felt encouraged*
Mrs. Giamoni	• *gave Wanda trash bags* • *encouraged Wanda* • *brought a rose bush*	• *Wanda felt supported* • *Mrs. G felt she'd helped Wanda* • *the lot was beautiful*
Ms. Jones, school librarian	• *gave Wanda information* • *brought muffins and a rose bush*	• *Wanda felt encouraged* • *everyone had food* • *the lot looked beautiful*
Mr. Sanchez, butcher	• *gave Wanda water* • *brought a rose bush* • *watered the rose bushes*	• *Wanda felt successful* • *Mr. Sanchez felt proud* • *the lot was beautiful*

Demonstrate sorting of contributions

➤ Duplicate a copy of the four cards on *Sample activities* (Blackline Master #4) for use in a class demonstration. Cut out the cards, and draw two columns on the board with the headings: "Contribution – YES" and "Contribution – NO." Read one of the cards from Blackline Master #4 and ask students whether the person in each situation is contributing or not to family or community (i.e., Does the person's action make a positive difference to someone else?). Place the card in the appropriate column on the board. Model providing reasons by pointing out the positive result (e.g., the woman can rest and the yard looks better) or the lack of positive difference for someone else (e.g., the person is only helping himself or herself).

bias

sorting

making a contribution

Sample activities
Blackline Master #4

Your neighbour's lawn is getting long. She has been sick and cannot cut it. You cut the lawn for her so she can relax and get better.

You just bought a new bike so you can have a better chance of winning the race.

Marcie loves hockey. Whenever she goes to the ice rink, she dreams of becoming a famous hockey player.

Jatinder loves riding horses. Jatinder's neighbour, Mrs. Lee, lets him ride her horse and, in

Sort contribution cards

➤ When students understand the concept of a contribution, distribute one copy of *Activity cards* (Blackline Master #5) and an enlarged copy (11 x 17) of *Is it a contribution?* (Blackline Master #6) to each pair of students. Instruct students to cut out the cards on Blackline Master #5. Students should read each card and decide whether the action is a contribution or not. They are to glue each card in the appropriate column on Blackline Master #6 and to provide a reason for the decision in the space beneath each card. Point out that students may be unsure whether or not some actions are contributions. In this case, ask students to glue the cards on the back of Blackline Master #6 and provide a reason beneath the card.

Activity cards
Blackline Master #5

People gave money, clothes and food to the Brown family because they lost everything in a fire.

Everyone in town gave money to build a new sports arena.

I really like watching television when I do my homework or when I read a book.

My class tried to make sure that all new students felt safe and happy during their first week of school.

On Saturday my family meets at the local park for a baseball game.

I saved my money for weeks to buy a new toy.

Name:

Students babysitti could en

Is it a contribution?
Blackline Master #6

Contribution – YES	Contribution – NO
Reason:	Reason:
Reason:	Reason:
Reason:	Reason:
Reason:	Reason:
Reason:	Reason:

Share decisions

➤ When students have completed the activity, examine each situation and compare students' decisions and reasons. Discuss those examples that are borderline contributions, using them to help students appreciate the contexts within which actions may or may not contribute to others.

Session Two   *Blackline Master #7*

Explore significance of contributions

➤ Remind students that a contribution involves making a positive difference to someone else. Discuss with students how they would decide that one action contributed more to a family or community than another action. As described below, use examples from the activities listed on the cards the previous day to teach about the relative significance of a contribution.

criteria for significant contribution

- *Importance of the need.* Invite students to compare the significance of giving clothes and money to the Brown family with the contribution of pleasure derived from the rose garden. Alternatively, ask students to imagine that the town had given money for a children's hospital instead of a sports arena. Would the contribution have been greater? Use these examples to suggest that the contribution may be greater if it meets a more important need (clothing or health as opposed to pleasure).

- *Number of people affected.* Invite students to imagine that the free babysitting service allowing parents to enjoy the school fair had been extended to all parents in the city. Would the contribution have been greater? Similarly, if clothes had been offered to more families than just the Brown family, would the contribution have been greater? Use these examples to suggest that the contribution may be greater if more people benefit from it.

- *Length of time of the effect.* Invite students to imagine that the plan to help new students feel safe during their first week had been extended for a longer period of time, perhaps for new students' first month at school. Would the contribution have been greater? Use this example to suggest that the contribution may be greater if the benefit lasts a longer period of time.

Illustrate the criteria

➤ Pose several examples and model for the class how to judge the significance of a contribution, using the agreed-upon criteria. Record students' ideas in a chart similar to the one following.

Making a contribution

Activity	What kind of benefit? (What needs are met?)	How many people benefit?	How long do people benefit?
• *picking up a single piece of garbage on the street*	• *makes person feel good* • *helps to keep other people healthy*	• *all the people who walk by*	• *a short time– if it was only done once*
• *sending money to poor people every month*	• *makes person feel good* • *helps to keep people from being hungry*	• *all the people who receive the money*	• *a long time— as long as the person sends the money*

After discussing each contribution in light of the criteria, ask students to decide whether the action contributes "a lot," "some," or "a little." Invite students to explain their decision by mentioning how well the criteria for a significant contribution are met.

Present the critical challenge

➤ The activity sheets on *Making a contribution* (Blackline Master #7A– B) contain eight situations where individuals are making contributions to others. Depending on the difficulty your students are likely to encounter, you may want to complete the first sheet (Blackline Master #7A) as a class or in groups of two or three, and ask students individually to complete the second sheet (Blackline Master #7B). Regardless of how you distribute the work, it may be helpful to read aloud each situation and allow students time to discuss or think about their answers before proceeding with the next situation. For each situation, pose the critical question:

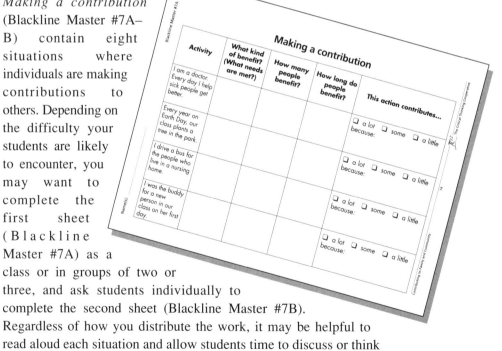

> *Are the people in this story contributing a lot, some, or a little to their family or community?*

➤ When students have completed the activity, invite them to share their decisions and their reasons. What similarities did students notice among those who contributed a lot to the community (many of these have jobs that involve them in contributing to the community).

Evaluation　　　　　　　　　*Blackline Master #8*

Assess community contributions

➤ Assess students' understanding of people's contributions to one another using the rubric *Assessing community contributions* (Blackline Master #8). The sources of evidence and the two criteria for this assessment are listed below:

- use students' responses to the class discussion and their answers to *Is it a contribution?* (Blackline Master #6) to assess students' ability to distinguish actions that contribute to others from those that do not;

- use students' responses to the class discussion and their answers to *Making a contribution* (Blackline Master #7A–B) to assess their ability to judge the significance of contributions to others.

Reaching the "basic understanding" level on the rubric may be appropriate for primary students who are new to the study of community.

References

Brisson, Pat. (2000). *Wanda's Roses* (illustrated by Maryann Cocca-Leffler). Honesdale, PA: Boyds Mills Press. (ISBN 1-56397-136-4)

Contributions in pictures

Critical Challenge

Critical task
Find the clues for what, where, who and why in the photograph and then offer your conclusions for each question.

Overview
In this challenge, students learn to extract information from photographs as they extend their understanding of the different community helpers and the contributions each makes. Students take on the role of detective in looking for clues in photographs depicting various community helpers in order to answer the questions: what, where, who and why. They then use their findings to explain how the person depicted in the photograph is contributing to the community.

Objectives

Broad understanding
Different roles in the community contribute in various ways to meeting community needs.

Requisite tools

Background knowledge
- knowledge of community services and needs

Criteria for judgment
- criteria for explaining a picture (e.g., based on information in the picture, uses a lot of clues)

Critical thinking vocabulary
- clue and conclusion

Thinking strategies
- 4W chart (what, where, who and why)

Habits of mind
- attention to detail

Suggested Activities

bias

clue and
conclusion

**Introduce clue
and conclusion**

➤ Ask if anyone in the class knows what a "clue" is. Offer several of the examples of clues suggested below and invite the class to reach a conclusion:

Here's my clue about...	**What is your conclusion?**
• *how I am feeling (cross your arms and look nasty)*	• *sad* • *mad*
• *what I am thinking about: "it has something to do with lunch"*	• *food* • *eating* • *time off*
• *what I am going to do tonight (mime typing on a computer)*	• *work on computer* • *play a video game*
• *my favourite activity (mime reading a book, or skiing)*	• *reading* • *skiing*

After several examples, help students to suggest words to define the two concepts:

* *clues* are hints or pieces of information that help you find out something;

* *conclusions* are answers or ideas that you think of because of a clue.

**Invite students
to suggest clues**

➤ Suggest several sample conclusions and invite students to offer clues that might lead to these conclusions:

My conclusion is...	**What clues might make me think this?**
• *that you are feeling happy*	• *smiling* • *laughing* • *having fun*
• *that you want to say something to me*	• *raising hand* • *trying to get attention* • *call your name*
• *that you are hungry*	• *eating* • *asking for food*

**Introduce
picture study**

➤ Indicate to the class that clues are not just in words, but that people get clues by looking at pictures. Explain that police officers and detectives study photographs for clues about who someone is and what they might be doing. Display an overhead transparency of *Picture #1* (Blackline Master #9) or distribute a copy of the picture to each pair of students. Explain that the class will be "community" detectives— trying to find out about everyone in the community and what they do, where they do it and why. As good detectives, students will "take one step at a time" and "they won't jump to conclusions." Explain that these phrases mean that students will answer one question before moving to the next question and that they will look for clues before coming to a conclusion. Create the outline of a chart by labeling the first column "Questions" and the second column "Clues." Print "What is the person doing?" in the question column and ask students to look for clues to the answer.

attention to detail

4W chart

Picture #1   Blackline Master #9

Write their clues in the second column. If students suggest a conclusion instead of a clue, do not write it down, but ask what they see in the picture that encourages them to think that the person is doing this (e.g., Why do you think the person is selling fruit and not selling meat or newspapers? Why do you think the person is selling fruit and not giving it away?). Collect student clues and offer some of your own for the "what" question. Then create a third column with the label "Conclusions." Record students' suggested conclusions and add some of your own. Encourage students to locate additional clues in support of the conclusions they offer. Repeat this procedure with the other three questions until you have created a chart similar to the following.

Studying the picture

Questions	Clues	Conclusions
What is the person doing?	• *lots of fruit* • *prices on the fruit* • *holding a knife* • *lots of empty boxes*	• *selling fruit* • *taking care of the fruit—cleaning, getting rid of rotten fruit* • *replacing the fruit that has been sold*
Where is this? (What is the place?)	• *stalls for fruit* • *cars* • *sidewalk* • *not much space*	• *a small grocery or fruit store* • *at the outside section*
Who is the person?	• *wearing an apron* • *holding a knife* • *working in a fruit store*	• *grocer* • *manager or clerk in the fruit department*
Why is the person doing it? (What needs is the person meeting?)	• *prices on fruit* • *lots of different fruit* • *holding a knife*	• *making money—is not giving the fruit away* • *providing food for people* • *making people happy by giving them the type of food they want* • *protecting heath by removing the rotten fruit*

Reinforce needs

➤ Encourage students to see the last question "Why is the person doing it?" as an invitation to explain what needs this person is meeting, both for himself and also for others in the community. It may be helpful to draw attention to the needs of people in a family and community. You may want to invite students to brainstorm basic needs or simply provide them with a list such as the following

knowledge of community needs

Basic family and community needs
- food
- health
- safety
- learning
- belonging
- fun
- earn a living
- ability to move about

Present practice challenge

➤ Arrange for students to practice studying another picture by distributing a copy of *Picture #2* (Blackline Master #10) and a copy of Studying pictures (Blackline Master #11) to each pair of students. Present the critical task:

Find the clues for what, where, who and why in the photograph and then offer your conclusions for each question.

Ask students to look at the picture for clues to the "what" question. They are to record these in words or simple drawings in the "Clues" box on Blackline Master #11. Review as a class the clues that students found for the first question. Invite students to add any clues to their chart that they had not already noticed. Then discuss as a class the conclusions that might be reached about the "what" question. Invite students to record these answers in the "Conclusions" box on their sheet. Repeat this procedure until the clues and conclusions to the remaining three questions have been addressed. With the final question, encourage students to discuss why the person is acting in light of the needs that he may help to meet. For example, the taxi driver may be helping people meet their health needs by providing emergency service to people who must get to a hospital. Collect the completed charts to determine how well students understand the task.

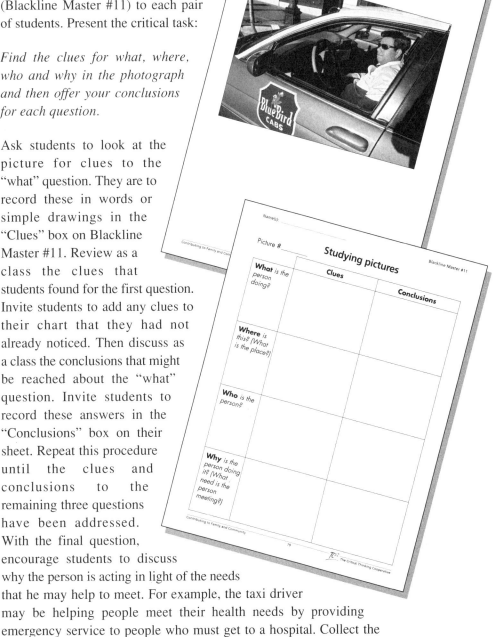

Prepare for picture study

➤ Duplicate sufficient copies of each of the remaining eight pictures (Blackline Masters #12–19) so that each pair of students will have one or more pictures to study. If you want each pair of students to study two pictures, you would need to duplicate three copies of each of the following pictures to accommodate a class of 24 students:

- sales clerk: *Picture #3* (Blackline Master #12)
- shoe repair: *Picture #4* (Blackline Master #13)
- street performer: *Picture #5* (Blackline Master #14)
- restaurant chef: *Picture #6* (Blackline Master #15)
- security guard: *Picture #7* (Blackline Master #16)
- car salesperson: *Picture #8* (Blackline Master #17)
- hair stylist: *Picture #9* (Blackline Master #18)
- street bottle/can collector: *Picture #10* (Blackline Master #19)

Also duplicate multiple copies of the 4W chart (Blackline Master #11) so that each pair of students will have a chart for every picture you want them to study.

Present additional challenges

➤ Direct those pairs of students who successfully completed the practice challenge to work independently on a picture they select from the above collection of pictures. When completed, quickly review their work before directing them to select a new picture to study. In the meanwhile, gather those students who struggled with the initial practice challenge into a group and repeat the practice procedure using one of the less challenging pictures (Pictures #4, 8–9). When students in this group are able to work on the task with a partner, give them a new picture and a 4W chart for use in completing the critical challenge. Encourage all students to find as many clues as they can and to use the clues to decide on their conclusions for each question.

criteria for explanation

Session Three   *Blackline Master #2B*

Share findings

➤ When students have completed their picture studies, on the board create a chart such as the one below. Invite students to share their findings in summary form. For each photograph, ask for volunteers to identify what they have learned about communities by connecting the 4W questions to the features of a community.

knowledge of community

Features of a community

	People (who)	Place (where)	Activities (what)	Needs met (why)
#1				
#2				
#3				

Add to the wall map

➤ OPTIONAL: Encourage students to draw pictures of the new people, places, things and activities they have learned about during this photo study. Since the drawings will go on the giant wall map of their own community, students must check that these features are actually found in their community. Provide copies of Blackline Master #2B for students to use in drawing their pictures. Ask students to introduce their features to the rest of the class as their drawings are attached to the map.

Evaluation   *Blackline Master #20*

Assess the picture study

➤ Assess students' ability to draw conclusions from pictures using the rubric *Assessing picture studies* (Blackline Master #20). The sources of evidence and the two criteria for this assessment are listed below:

- use students' responses to the class discussion and their answers to *Studying pictures* (Blackline Master #11) to assess students' ability to distinguish clues from conclusions;

- use students' responses to the class discussion and their answers to *Studying pictures* (Blackline Master #11) to assess students' ability to recognize relevant clues and to draw conclusions from them.

Reaching the "basic understanding" level on the rubric may be appropriate for primary students who are new to the study of community.

Is this a community?

4

Critical Challenge

Critical task

Decide whether the people in the sketch and story are a community or not.

Overview

In this challenge, students learn that a community, in the true sense of the word, is not characterized by the presence of any particular people, places or things, but by a special kind of activity (positive interactions among the members). As an introduction, students observe three role-plays by older students, each illustrating a different theme—no interactions, positive interactions and negative interactions. Students then role-play these different forms of interaction in a typical classroom situation. Based on these experiences, students learn that a community requires interaction among members and the interactions must help people meet their needs. Students are given a number of stories with accompanying drawings about various groups of people. They learn to identify the people, places, things and activities in the scenes and to sort this information according to possible conclusions. After a practice example, students determine which of these group situations represent a community (mutually beneficial interactions) and which do not.

Objectives

Broad understanding

Positive interactions among people are the defining features of a community.

Requisite tools

Background knowledge
- knowledge of types of community interactions

Criteria for judgment
- criteria for a community (e.g., a group of people whose interactions help meet one another's needs)

Critical thinking vocabulary
- clue and conclusion

Thinking strategies
- sorting
- information chart

Habits of mind
- attention to detail

Suggested Activities

Pre-planning

➤ To introduce this challenge, arrange for a few intermediate students to perform three simple scenarios for your class. In all three role-plays, the students are to play the same game (e.g., marbles, cards) but perform them each time with a different twist:

- *first role-play:* students play the game separately with their backs to each other (no interaction);

- *second role-play:* students play the game together in a very collaborative manner (interacting with each other);

- *third role-play:* students play the game together in an uncooperative manner (negative interaction).

Make arrangements with an intermediate classroom teacher and three students in advance to allow these students an opportunity to practice the role-play.

Session One

Present role-plays

➤ Remind students that previously they had identified many features of a community. Explain that a group of intermediate students will role-play three situations to help the class learn more about what makes a community. As they watch each situation, encourage students to look for the people, places, things and activities that are present. Without much comment, ask the intermediate students to perform the three scenarios for about 30 seconds each.

Discuss role-plays

➤ When students have observed the role-plays, ask them to comment on what was similar and different about the three situations. Begin with "people" and ask students to identify who was involved in each situation. Proceed with the three other features of a community. Record students' comments on the chalkboard, creating a chart such as the one below. In the discussion, guide students to understand that the people, place and things did not change, but the activities did.

Features of a community

	People	**Places**	**Things**	**Activities**
1	*three students*	*classroom*	*marbles*	*playing game by themselves, not playing together, not talking to each other, may not be having very much fun*
2	*three students*	*classroom*	*marbles*	*playing game together, talking together, having fun*
3	*three students*	*classroom*	*marbles*	*playing together, arguing, fighting, not having fun*

Introduce kinds of interactions

➤ Ask students to explain in their own words the differences among the activities in the three situations. While it is not essential that you use the exact terminology, draw out the following ideas:

knowledge of community interactions

- *no interaction:* in the first situation, students did not have anything to do with each other—they did not interact with each other; they did not bother each other or be nice to each other;

- *positive interaction:* in the second situation, students had a lot to do with each other—they interacted with each other; they were nice to each other, and did not bother each other;

- *negative interaction:* in the third situation, students had a lot to do with each other—they interacted with each other; but they did not help each other, they only bothered each other.

Practice role-playing

➤ Ask every student to take out a book. Explain that you want them to show you what it looks like when students interact with each other in different ways, just as the older students demonstrated earlier. Ask everyone to read their book without any interaction. Coach students so that no one is even looking or smiling at each other. After a brief while, ask everyone to read their book while interacting positively with the students around them. Coach students on what this would look like (e.g., sharing ideas, pointing to each others' books, reading to each other, asking questions). Finally, ask students—either the entire class or one table at a time—to show without hitting, shoving or throwing what reading would look like while interacting negatively with the students around them (e.g., making noise so others cannot read, criticizing their books, putting a hand over the page). Discuss how students felt in each situation. Ask students to indicate which situation is the best situation if everyone is to learn and feel good about themselves and about other students. Suggest that when people truly are a community, they interact in positive ways to help each other meet their needs.

Session Two   *Blackline Masters #21–22*

Introduce picture and story study

➤ Explain to students that they are going to learn about a group of people. Display an overhead transparency of the picture and story of *The Brown family* (Blackline Master #21) and distribute a copy to each pair of students. Invite students to again assume a detective role. Their task is to decide if the Brown family is a "true" community. The students' first step will be to determine the features of a community present in the drawing and the story of the Brown family. Create a chart such as the one below on the board or on a large sheet of paper on the wall.

Features of the Brown family

People (who)	Places (where)	Things (what they have)	Activities (what they do)

➤ Begin with the drawing. Isolate one section of the overhead transparency by covering the other parts of the picture with paper. Ask students to identify what they notice in the visible section about the people, places, things and activities. Record each observation on an index card or slip of paper (or ask students to do this) and place the cards in the appropriate columns on the chart. Inquire what difference it made in students' observations when you covered all but one part of the picture. Did students notice features that they had not seen before? Provide materials for each student to make a tube or distribute toilet paper rolls to every student. Invite students to look at different sections of the picture through the tube to help them see the detail. As students notice features, either you or the students should record their observations on cards and attach them to the chart.

attention to detail

The Brown family

Blackline Master #21

The Brown family lives in an apartment on First Street. Mrs. Brown goes to work to earn money so that she can pay rent for a place to live. Then she can also buy clothes, food, medicine, books, tools and other things her family needs for school and for play. The neighbour looks after the two children after school until Mrs. Brown gets home from work. The children help by feeding the dog, keeping their rooms tidy and drying the dishes. On holidays, Mrs. Brown and her two children play games, tell each other stories, and go to the beach, the library, the museum and to baseball and soccer games at the park. The family also likes to swim at the city pool on the weekend. Sometimes the Brown family has a BBQ with their friends.

Contributing to Family and Community

89

JC² The Critical Thinking Cooperative

Read the text

➤ When students have no further visual observations to share, read aloud the story to the class. Ask students to identify new features. Reread the story and ask students to stop you by raising their hand any time they hear new information about the features of the Brown family. Record these on cards and attach them to the chart.

Review criteria for a community

➤ Remind students of the previous day's role-plays and what they learned about the qualities of a "true" community. Invite students to share their ideas. Draw out two qualities of a community:

• people interact with one another—they work and play with each other;

• the interactions are positive contributions—people help each other meet their needs.

Present these two criteria in the form of questions that students are to use when deciding whether or not the Brown family is a community:

• Is everyone interacting? (Are people working and playing with each other?)

• Is everyone contributing? (Are people helping each other meet their needs?)

criteria for community

information chart

Write the two questions on the board and ask students to suggest possible answers to them. As illustrated below, beneath each question, add the words "yes," "no," and "maybe."

Is everyone interacting?
(Are people working and playing with each other?)

YES	MAYBE	NO

Is everyone contributing?
(Are people helping each other meet their needs?)

YES	MAYBE	NO

Identify possible conclusions

➤ Invite the class to use the information from the "Features of the Brown Family" chart to answer the questions mentioned above. Suggest that this information provides clues to the answers. Begin by asking if students see any information (clues) that might suggest the conclusion that "Yes, everyone in the Brown family is interacting" Ask students to select these cards from the features chart and place them in the "Yes" column under "Is everyone interacting?" Ask if any clues suggest that the Browns may or may not be interacting with each other. If any clues suggest these conclusions, take these cards from the features chart and place them in the appropriate columns. Repeat the procedure for the second criteria—"Is everyone contributing?" If students notice that information already placed on the conclusions chart applies to this question, create a second index card to attach under the appropriate option. Leave those pieces of information that are not relevant to any of the possible conclusions on the features chart.

clue and conclusion

sorting

Pose the critical challenge

➤ When all relevant information (clues) has been placed beneath each conclusions option, present the critical task:

Decide whether the [Brown family is]…a community or not.

Ask students to decide which conclusion is most suggested by the clues: Is the Brown family a community: Yes? No? or Maybe? Point out that everyone need not reach the same conclusion. Ask several students to state their conclusion and give a reason.

Debrief activity

➤ Discuss with students the difficulties experienced during this activity, what was easy and what new things they learned about communities. Following the discussion, ask students to record their thoughts in their learning journal or on a copy of *Thinking about my learning* (Blackline Master #22). In the box at the bottom, ask students to draw a picture of the Brown family helping each other meet their needs. Review students' reflections prior to the next session.

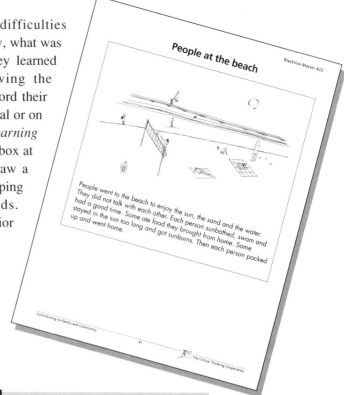

Session Three

Blackline Masters #23–25

Present practice challenge

➤ Announce to students that because of their successful detective work the previous day, they have been asked to find out whether another group of people is a community or not. Distribute a copy of *People at the beach* (Blackline Master #23) and a copy of both sheets of *What we see and hear* (Blackline Master #24A–B) to each pair of students.

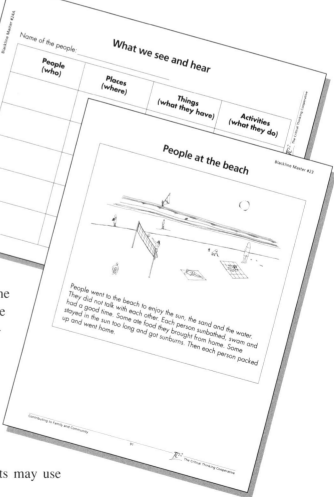

Focus on the drawing

➤ Ask students to look first at the drawing for information about the people, places, things and activities. Encourage students to use their tubes to help them notice details about the beach people. Instruct students to record this information in words or simple drawings—one piece of information per box—on Blackline Master #24A. Students may use the second sheet (Blackline Master #24B) if they need more space. After a short while, invite students to share their information about the people, places, things and activities with the rest of the class. As was done previously, record their suggestions on cards or paper which are then attached to a chart on the wall. Invite students to add any new information they see on the class chart to their own sheets.

Examine the story

➤ After the class has shared information from the story, read with students the text under the picture. Ask students to add any new information in the relevant boxes on Blackline Master #24. As before, share these ideas with the rest of the class by pasting cards or paper with the information to the class chart. Invite students to add any information to their own sheets that they had not already noticed.

Model making a decision

➤ Now that students have collected the information, they can sort it to see which conclusion is supported by each piece of information. Distribute an enlarged copy (11 x 17) of *Is this a community?* (Blackline Master #25A–B) to each pair of students. Walk students through the procedure of cutting out the information boxes on Blackline Master #24A–B; then sorting the slips of paper according to the conclusion each supports; and finally pasting them in the correct columns on Blackline Master #25A–B. Model the procedure by taking a slip of information from one student's chart and showing where it would be pasted on the conclusions sheet. After sorting and pasting the relevant slips of paper, each pair of students should then decide what overall conclusion is most consistent with the clues (yes, no or maybe). Students indicate their conclusion by placing a check in the appropriate box at the bottom of Blackline Master #25B. Remind students that everyone does not need to reach the same conclusion.

Debrief practice session

➤ Ask several students to indicate what conclusion they reached and to give a reason. Discuss any difficulties experienced during this activity. Collect the completed charts on Blackline Master #25A–B to determine how well students can match clues to the implied conclusion.

Prepare for picture study

➤ Duplicate sufficient copies of each of the remaining eight group scenarios (Blackline Masters #26–33) so that each pair of students will have one or more groups to study. If you want each pair of students to study two scenarios, duplicate three copies of each of the following to accommodate a class of 24 students:

• *A hermit* (Blackline Master #26)

• *People in a mining town* (Blackline Master #27)

• *People at a mountain resort* (Blackline Master #28)

• *People living on a small island* (Blackline Master #29)

• *Families at the beach* (Blackline Master #30)

• *People living in a big city* (Blackline Master #31)

• *The O'Hara family* (Blackline Master #32)

• *People in a school* (Blackline Master #33)

Also duplicate multiple copies of Blackline Master #24A–B and Blackline Master #25A–B (enlarged to 11 x 17) so that each pair of students has the charts to record information about the scenario and the charts to match the cut-out clues with the conclusions.

Present additional challenges

➤ Review any difficulties from the previous day. Invite students to continue with their quest to determine the different kinds of groups that qualify as communities. Again present the critical task:

> *Decide whether the people in the sketch and story are a community or not.*

Direct those pairs of students who successfully completed the practice challenge to work independently on a group selected from the above collection of scenarios. When completed, quickly review their work before directing them to select a new scenario. Meanwhile, gather together those students who struggled with the initial practice challenge. Repeat the practice procedure using one of the less challenging scenarios (Blackline Masters #32–33). When these students are able to work on the task with a partner, give them a new scenario and the necessary Blackline Masters (#24A–B; #25A–B enlarged). Encourage all students to find as much information as they can from each drawing and story, and to use this information to decide whether their group is a community or not.

Share findings

➤ When every student has analyzed the allotted scenarios, ask students to indicate the conclusions they reached for each situation they analyzed. Record each pair's conclusions by placing a check mark on a chart such as the one listed below. Discuss those situations where students disagree about the conclusions or where the conclusions are "may be."

Is it a community?

	Is a community	Is not a community	May be a community
People at the beach		✓✓✓✓✓	
Hermit		✓✓✓✓	✓✓
People in a mining town	✓✓✓✓✓		

Debrief activity

➤ Discuss with students their difficulties in reaching a conclusion, what was easy and what new things they learned about communities. Following the discussion, ask students to record their thoughts in a learning journal or on a copy of Blackline Master #22.

Assess community features

➤ Assess students' ability to identify the different community features in various group scenarios using the first criterion on the rubric *Assessing community features* (Blackline Master #3). The sources of evidence are students' responses in class discussions and as recorded on *What we see and hear* (Blackline Master #24A–B). Reaching the "basic understanding" level on the rubric may be appropriate for many primary students who are new to the study of community.

Assess understanding of community

➤ Assess students' ability to decide when a group is a community using the rubric *Assessing understanding of community* (Blackline Master #34). Use students' responses in class discussions and recorded on *Is this a community?* (Blackline Master #25) to assess their ability to provide relevant information in support of various conclusions and to use this information to decide whether or not a group is a community. Reaching the "basic understanding" level on the rubric may be appropriate for many primary students who are new to the study of community.

Blackline Master #34

Assessing understanding of community

Supports conclusions with information	Pre-recognition	Partial recognition	Basic understanding	Extended understanding	Sophisticated understanding
Decides whether a group is a community	Does not understand what is meant when asked to provide information to support differing conclusions.	Understands what is asked, but has difficulty providing relevant information to support even very obvious conclusions.	Provides only the most obvious pieces of information to support conclusions.	Provides several generally obvious pieces of information to support conclusions.	Provides a range of obvious and less obvious pieces of information to support conclusions.
	Does not understand what it means to decide whether or not groups of people are communities.	Understands what is asked, but has difficulty deciding whether or not groups of people are communities even in very obvious situations.	Decides in the most obvious situations whether or not groups of people are communities, but cannot explain why they meet the identified criteria.	Decides in obvious situations whether or not groups of people are communities, offering very simple explanations why they meet the identified criteria.	Decides in a range of situations whether or not groups of people are communities, explaining in own words why they meet the identified criteria.

Comments:

Name(s):

Our own community adventure

5

Critical Challenge

Critical task
Create your own community adventure story using all of your community place and service cards.

Overview
The focus of this challenge turns more directly to the places and roles within the students' surrounding community. Students begin by identifying the places and community roles represented in a book, *On the Town: A Community Adventure* by Judith Caseley. Students are then given cards identifying many different places. Their job is to decide whether these places are found in their own community. Students play two versions of a game matching these places with the services and people (roles) that they could expect to find at each site. Finally, students write their own community adventure story, accommodating two places and two services identified on cards they have been randomly assigned.

Objectives

Broad understanding
Many people in roles within students' own community work to meet the needs of others.

Requisite tools

Background knowledge
- knowledge of places, services and roles in students' own community
- understanding of role

Criteria for judgment
- criteria for community story (e.g., uses all the cards, correctly matches roles, places and services)

Critical thinking vocabulary

Thinking strategies
- story line frame

Habits of mind

Suggested Activities

Introduce the story

➤ Introduce the idea of learning more about the places and roles in the students' community using the story *On the Town: A Community Adventure* by Judith Caseley. This book tells of Charlie's travels about his town in response to a class assignment to find out about his community. He makes notes about the many places, the people at each place and the activities that occupy them. *Franklin's Neighbourhood* by Paulette Bourgeois would also be a suitable book for our purposes. It tells of Franklin's adventures in response to a class project to identify what he likes best about his community. Introduce *On the Town: A Community Adventure* with the following pre-reading activities:

- discuss what makes something an adventure;

- predict the kind of adventure that might happen in a community;

- look at the cover pictures contained in the letters of the title for clues about Charlie's adventure.

Read the story and ask students to listen for the places and people encountered on Charlie's adventure.

Identify community roles and places

➤ After reading the story, discuss the following questions:

- Why did the author call the book "a community adventure"?

- Were students' predicted ideas about an adventure the same as the author's?

- What places and people did Charlie discover on his community adventure?

Record students' answers to the last question in a two-column chart under the headings "Places" and "People/Roles." Use the discussion to explore the many different people/roles found at a given place in the community. When the text refers to the first name of a person, ask students for the name of the job performed by the person (e.g. Joe is the police officer). Explain that a role is the job that people have within different places in the community or family. Remind students that they have several roles: at school, they are students; at home, they are brothers or sisters and sons or daughters. Encourage students to look at the pictures in the story for roles present at each place, but not mentioned by Charlie. Remind students to look for clues in the pictures when identifying these roles.

understanding of role

Places in Charlie's community	People/Roles in Charlie's community
school	• *Charlie's teacher* • *other teachers* • *music teacher* • *art teacher* • *students* • *custodian* • *parents*
park	• *garbage collector* • *people sitting and walking in the park*

Identify actual places in students' community

➤ Explain to students that they are now going to think of the roles and places in their own community. Begin by drawing attention to the list of places in Charlie's community. Briefly discuss which of these places are found in the community in which the students live. Duplicate one copy of the sheets of cards on *Community places* (Blackline Master #35A–D). Cut out the 48 cards and give one to each student. Ask students to read their card (with a partner and, if needed, with your help) and decide whether the place on the card can be found in their own community. Once students have discussed their answer with a partner, they are to read their card aloud and state whether or not it can be found in their community.

> **Community places** — Blackline Master #35A
>
> | animal hospital | bakery |
> | barber shop | restaurant |
> | video store | garage |
> | church | grocery store |
> | bank | post office |
> | fire hall | newspaper |
>
> Contributing to Family and Community   105   The Critical Thinking Cooperative

Record community places

➤ If you are using a giant map, after students read their card, temporarily attach any cards indicating places that are found in your community in the approximate locations on the map. (The cards can be replaced with student drawings in a later challenge.) If the site is not within the scope of your map, place it along the map's edge. If you do not know where the place is located or if a student incorrectly identifies a place as a site within your community, explain to the class that you have never visited this place and you will need their help in deciding where it belongs on the map. Their "homework" for next day will be

knowledge of own community

to discover where these unknown places are found in the community. When students announce that a place is not found in your community (even if they are incorrect), add the card to an adjacent list titled, "Places in other communities." If you are not using a giant wall map, place cards that would have been attached to the community map to a list titled, "Places in our community." Over the next few days as opportunities arise, encourage students to rethink any incorrect decisions about places in their community.

Anticipate next class

➤ For additional "homework," students are to observe in their neighbourhood and talk to their parents about other places in the community that were not included on the cards. Ask students to add these to the map (or to the list) at the start of the next session.

Session Two   Blackline Master #36

Play the "Where would I go?" game

➤ To help students learn about the places in their community, play a game called "Where would I go if...?" Practice as a class, by suggesting the following examples and asking for answers from student volunteers:

knowledge of community services

• Where would I go if I was sick?

• Where would I go if I needed to get my teeth checked?

• Where would I go if I had a sick cat?

If desired, invite students to point to the appropriate place card either on the map or on one of the lists. Explain that this help may be found in more than one place. When students understand the task, cut out the cards on *Help cards* (Blackline Master #36A–B), eliminating any services not found in your community. Distribute a different card to each student one at a time. Invite the student to read the card and then indicate the place that would provide the help. For example, "If I wanted a haircut. I will go to the (barbershop)."

Help cards   Blackline Master #36A

I had a toothache.	I wanted a haircut.
I wanted to find out about dinosaurs.	I wanted to see a funny movie.
I needed to get my noisy car fixed.	I had a flat tire.
I wanted a loaf of bread.	I wanted something to eat right away.
I needed a new pair of boots.	I had to mail a parcel to my grandma.
I had a sore ear.	I fell and hurt my arm.
I needed to get medicine for my cat.	I found a stray dog.

Contributing to Family and Community

109

**Add "Who would I see?"
dimension**

➤ After playing through the 30 or so *Help* cards or when every student
has had a turn, add a new twist to the game. Invite students to
suggest "who" (what roles) they might expect to see at each place.
Indicate that the new game is called "Where would I go and who
would I see if…?" Practice as a class, by suggesting the following
examples and asking for answers from student volunteers:

- Where would I go and who would I see if I was sick?

- Where would I go and who would I see if I needed to get my
teeth checked?

- Where would I go and who would I see if I had a sick cat?

After accepting the most likely answers to these questions, invite
students to suggest additional roles that might also be found at these
places. For example, at a dentist's office, students are likely to find a
dentist, a nurse (dental hygienist) and a secretary (receptionist).
Encourage students to name more than one role if they are able. Go
around the class, playing the game with this new twist. Make a note
of any community places where students are unable to mention a
role. Assign as "homework" the task of identifying roles that might
be found at these less well-known places. More generally, encourage
students to ask someone at home for the names of additional roles
that might be found at a place the student was assigned in the game.

Session Three   *Blackline Masters #35–37*

Re-play the game

➤ OPTIONAL: If students enjoyed the game "Where would I go and
who would I see if…?" from the previous day or have found new
roles to add to community places, play the game again.

**Introduce
the community
adventure story**

➤ Remind students of
Charlie's community
adventure in *On The
Town.* Ask students to
recall some of the
places, people (roles)
and events that he
encountered. If
necessary, reread the
book or refer back
to the chart created
from the story.
Explain to the
class that they
are going to
write their own
community adventure story. If
you want this activity to be done
individually, duplicate two copies of each of the sheets
of community places (Blackline Master #35A–B) and help cards

Blackline Master #37A

My own community adventure

I woke up one morning and

so I decided to go to _____ *needed help*

when I got there I met _____ *community place*

and then _____ *roles*

_____ *how they helped*

1.

I just got home when _____

I ran to _____

Once inside I saw _____

I was so happy _____

Name(s):

(Blackline Master #36A–B). If the activity is to be done in pairs, one copy of these sheets will suffice. You can make the task somewhat easier by duplicating the help and place cards on different coloured paper. You can make the task considerably easier by using only help cards and no community place cards. Remove any cards that do not apply to the local community or that have posed difficulties for students during the game. Distribute two place cards and two help cards to each student (or pair of students). For the easiest challenge, distribute four help cards. Also distribute an enlarged copy (11 x 17) of both sheets of *My own community adventure* (Blackline Master #37A–B) to each student or pair of students.

Explain the story line frame

➤ Show students how to use the cards they have been given and the story line frame to create their own community adventure story. Write the following story line frame on the blackboard, leaving sufficient room to attach community place and help cards in the blank spaces. Read the words of the frame and then select a help card. Place the help card in the first blank space and ask students to tell you where you would go if you needed this help. Record this in the second blank space. Then ask who you might find at this place and record these answers in the third space. Finally, ask students what these people do to help you get what you want or need. Record this in the last blank space. Repeat this procedure once or twice more with other help cards, then select a community place card. Ask students where they think you should put this card. Walk students though the procedure for creating the adventure using the place card as the prompt. Assist students by asking the question, "If I had to go to a (dentist), what kind of help do you think I might need?"

story line

I woke up one morning and _____ *needed help* _____

so I decided to go to _____ *community place* _____

when I got there I met _____ *roles* _____

and then _____ *how they helped* _____

Present the critical challenge

➤ When students are ready to begin creating their story, present the critical task:

criteria for community story

> *Create your own community adventure story using all of your community place and service cards.*

➤ Remind students that they must use all fours cards (one for each adventure) and that the places should match with the roles and services in each adventure. Emphasize that students are to use the words from only one card for each frame. Suggest that students number the back of each card from #1 to #4 and that they match the card's number with the number on the story line (i.e., card #1 would be used to create adventure #1). If you colour-coded the cards, explain to students that the words from the help (blue) cards can only go on the first line and the words from the place (pink) cards can only go on the second line.

Share stories

Provide an opportunity for students to read their adventures to the entire class and also in small groups. If desired, as students read their story line trace the route that their adventures took them on the map.

Evaluation

Blackline Master #38

Assess community places and roles

➤ Assess students' knowledge of the roles and services associated with places in their community using the rubric *Assessing community places and roles* (Blackline Master #38). The sources of evidence for this assessment are students' responses during the games and their story line recorded on *My own community adventure* (Blackline Master #37A–B). Reaching the "basic understanding" level on the rubric may be appropriate for many primary students who are new to the study of community.

References

Bourgeois, Paulette. (1999). *Franklin's Neighbourhood* (illustrated by Brenda Clark). Toronto: Kids Can Press (ISBN 1-55074-704-5)

Caseley, Judith. (2002). *On The Town: A Community Adventure*. Harper Collins (ISBN 0-06-029584-8)

A most important contribution

6

Critical Challenge

Critical question

What is the most important contribution of the person in this role?

Overview

In this challenge, students learn about a particular community role or helper. Students gather information from interviews, field trips or picture books, about the contributions made by their allocated role. Based on their research, students select four important contributions and decide which one of these is their role's most important contribution towards meeting the diverse needs of people in the community. Students send a note of appreciation to a representative of their community role, acknowledging his or her help and expressing special thanks for making the most important contribution attached to this role. Students share their information with the rest of the class and draw pictures of various features associated with their role.

Objectives

Broad understanding

Many people contribute to meeting students' needs at home and in the community.

Requisite tools

Background knowledge
- knowledge of contributions related to roles
- knowledge of ways needs are met

Criteria for judgment
- criteria for important contribution (e.g., meets important needs, benefit is long lasting, reaches many people)

Critical thinking vocabulary

Thinking strategies
- guided research questions
- sorting

Habits of mind
- curiosity

Suggested Activities

Decide on research methods

➤ In this challenge, the information that students will need can be gathered through three methods:

- interviewing community personnel about their roles,

- visiting locations within their community,

- reading picture books about these roles.

You may want to select one option only, or adopt a combination of all three approaches. For example, you might take the class on one or two field trips, bring in a few other community helpers to be interviewed by the entire class, and assign students to read books about yet other community roles. Our approach in this challenge can be used equally well with interviews and book research. In fact, subject to availability of human and print resources, we suggest that each pair of students be allowed to choose a book or interview option. A substantial, but by no means adequate, list of books on a variety of community roles/places is included in References. Consult with a teacher-librarian for availability of these resources and for additional titles.

Plan for interviews

➤ OPTIONAL: If you propose interviews as an option, you will need to identify suitable people within the community (in time for Session Three), decide when and where the interviews will be conducted, and determine the support that students will need. In addition to contacting people you know in the community who may be willing to be interviewed, you may want to solicit parent volunteers. Consider whether to conduct the interviews at school in one or two after-hours sessions or to encourage parents to accompany their child to the interviewee's place of work. Consider arranging for parents or older student helpers to assist in recording interviewee responses. Confirm the willingness and availability of potential interviewees well in advance, and provide them with a copy of the questions prior to the interview. Obtain their address so a note of appreciation can be mailed to them.

Determine selection of roles

➤ Decide in advance whether you will allocate roles or allow students to select their own. We have assumed that students will work in pairs on this project. Encourage those students who want to focus on the same role to work together. Although it is not optimal, consider allowing more than one pair of students to research the same role. A significant limitation on students' choices may be availability of resources—especially if an interview is planned.

Explore needs

➤ OPTIONAL: The theme for this challenge is how various roles contribute to meeting community needs. If your students are unfamiliar with the ways in which basic community needs might be met, distribute a set of the help cards (Blackline Master #36A–B) and an enlarged copy of *Meeting basic needs* (Blackline Master #39A–B) to each group of three or four students. Review each of the needs, defining any terms that students may not understand. Ask each group to cut out the help cards and sort them according to the need (or needs) that describes the benefit that will follow if the help is provided. Students should then paste the cards beneath the appropriate need. For example, the help card about fixing a flat tire would be pasted on Blackline Master #39B beneath the need for people to get around. Some students may notice that some help cards may invoke more than one type of need. For example, getting help to learn to read and write will serve the need for learning, but also for making a living and, perhaps, for the need to have fun. In these cases, suggest that students paste the card under its most important need and also write a description of the help in a box beneath any other relevant need. Some help cards may not address any of the needs listed on Blackline Master #39A–B. In these cases, students may add new needs to the back of the chart or leave the cards off the chart altogether.

knowledge of needs

sorting

Build curiosity

➤ Ask students to think about places and roles in their community they would like to know more about. Perhaps students are curious about a certain role or place in their community. Discuss with students how they would know if they were curious. They may have had questions about certain roles or places during their discussion. Engender student curiosity by asking if they know much about a local place that may be particularly interesting or who in the community has special duties, such as deciding the names given to streets or the kinds of playground equipment placed in local parks.

curiosity

Discuss research questions

➤ Invite students to suggest questions they might want answered. In particular, encourage them to think of questions they might ask to better understand the contributions made by people in the community. Before announcing that students will conduct research, ask them to indicate three roles that they would like to learn more about. The sheet, *I am curious about…*(Blackline Master #40), may be useful for this purpose. Use this information to determine the amount of overlap in student interests and to identify needed resources. Explain to students that their ideas will help you prepare a list of questions.

Prepare research questions

➤ Before the next session, decide on questions to guide students' research. You may want to use the questions found on *Our book research* (Blackline Master #41A–B) and/or *Our interview* (Blackline Master #42A–B). The difference between these two forms is the manner in which questions are framed: in the former, they are framed as questions that students will ask of themselves in guiding their book research; in the latter, they are framed as questions that students will ask of an interviewee. In addition, we have left room for students to add a question of their own once they know the role they will be researching. You may prefer to create your own questions based on student suggestions. For the purposes of this challenge, we recommend that the core questions deal with each role's contributions.

**Explain research/
interview questions**

➤ Invite the class to consider where they might get answers to their questions about community roles. Guide students to the conclusion that they could ask people directly or read about them. Indicate that asking people prepared questions is called an interview. Whether students are asking people directly or looking things up in books, it is helpful to have questions to guide what to look for or ask about. Distribute an enlarged copy (11 x 17) of our interview questions (Blackline Master #42A–B) or the interview form you have developed to each student. Even if students will not be interviewing other role members, we suggest students interview each other. Not only will this teach students about the questions they will need to address in their research, it offers them the experience of interviewing someone and being interviewed. Read the questions and explain where students would record the information. Indicate that students should record more than "yes" or "no" answers by providing examples and details.

*guided research
questions*

Name(s)

Hello, _____

Our names are _____
Thank you for agreeing to answer our questions.

Our interview   Blackline Master #42A

Q.
What is your role or job in our community?   A.

Q.
Where do you work?   A.

We have been studying how people in our community help meet each other's needs.

Q.
In your role, do you help people LEARN?   A.

Contributing to Family and Community   119

**Conduct sample
interviews**

➤ Explain that as community members, everyone in the class has a role or job in the community—they are all students. Indicate that students will interview each other for two purposes: to learn about the questions that will guide their research of other community roles and to help students appreciate the contributions they make to the community. You may want to coach students on the kinds of contributions they make. Ask, for example, how they help others learn or contribute to fellow students' and family members' need to be safe and to feel as though they belong. Place students into pairs. Ask students to take turns interviewing each other, using the template both to guide their questions and to record the responses. It may be helpful to arrange for several students or parent volunteers to assist students in recording the responses. You may want to conduct these interviews in unison by reading aloud the first question and allowing time for students to respond and record, before proceeding with the second question and so on. Repeat this process to allow both students in each pair to be interviewed. Afterwards, invite a few students to share the information they collected.

Formalize research focus

➤ Using whatever allocation method you have planned, settle on the community role that each pair of students will research. Indicate whether any students (and, if so, which students) will be able to conduct their research by interview. Provide each pair of students with a fresh enlarged copy of the appropriate Blackline Master (#41A–B or 42A–B, or your own research/interview form). In partners, invite students to generate additional questions they might have about their community role.

Implement research gathering plan

➤ Try to arrange things so that any work at home or in the classroom for the interview and book research groups coincide. If interviews are scheduled, explain to students the plan for conducting them. Allow time for each pair of students to meet and practice prior to their scheduled interviews. For students conducting book-based research, arrange for the relevant books to be available in the classroom or school library. Encourage these students to look at the pictures as well as the words for clues to the answers to the questions. Reassure students that they may not be able to find answers to every question.

Session Four

Share information

➤ After all students have gathered their information, ask each pair to present its findings to the class. Instruct students to start by stating the role, the place where the person works and, if an interview was held, the person's actual name. Each partner should take turns reporting on the answers to the questions.

Select four important contributions

➤ Organize students according to the role they researched. Ask each pair to examine its completed research sheets (Blackline Masters #41A–B; #42A–B). Students are to select four important contributions of their role. Distribute four stars or other small stickers. Direct students to place stickers next to the role's four most important contributions. Remind students of the factors they considered when deciding important contributions in Critical Challenge #2:

criteria for important contributions

- meets important needs (some needs such as health and safety may be matters of life and death; others may be nice to have, but not as important);

- reaches many people (some contributions may help only a few people; others may help many people);

- benefits last a long time (some contributions may last a long time; others a very short time).

Encourage students to think of these three factors as they discuss the importance of each contribution.

Present critical challenge

➤ When students have identified four important contributions, present the critical question:

What is the most important contribution of people in this community role?

Remind students to think of the three questions mentioned above as they decide upon the single most important contribution.

Session Five — Blackline Masters #2, 43

Prepare note of appreciation

➤ Once each group has selected four important contributions and then chosen which of these is the most important, distribute an enlarged copy (11 x 17) of *Note of appreciation* (Blackline Master #43) to each pair of students. Explain that they will prepare and send a note of appreciation to the person they interviewed (or to a local representative of this role) to thank the person for his or her contributions to the community. Remind students to state the three important contributions in addition to the most important contribution. They should also state the need that the most important contribution helps to meet (e.g., safety, health). When the written part is completed, ask each student to draw a picture of the community helper making his or her most important contribution. Distribute a piece of paper approximately the size of the box on Master #43 to ensure that the pictures will fit on the note of appreciation. Let each pair of students choose which picture to paste in the box on the note of appreciation (and attach the other to the note) or suggest that students pick a number to decide. Send the notes when completed.

Note of appreciation — Blackline Master #43

To: _____
Role: _____
Place: _____

We appreciate many things that you do to help our community meet its needs:

1. _____
2. _____
3. _____

But we REALLY appreciate how you help the community meet its need to _____
when you _____
Thank you very, very much.
Signed _____

Add to the giant map

➤ OPTIONAL: Distribute a copy of Blackline Master #2B, used in the first lesson, to draw pictures of community features that students would most miss if they moved away. Ask each pair of students to collectively draw the four pictures depicting the person/role researched, the place where the person works, a thing used (piece of equipment) and an activity carried out. When completed, add these drawings to the giant community map.

Assess understanding of needs

➤ Assess students' knowledge of the various ways in which needs are met using the rubric *Assessing understanding of needs* (Blackline Master #44). The source of evidence is students' ability to sort the help cards according to need. Reaching the "basic understanding" level on the rubric may be appropriate for many primary students who are new to the study of community.

Blackline Master #44

Assessing understanding of needs

Knowledge of ways needs are met	Pre-recognition	Partial recognition	Basic understanding	Extended understanding	Sophisticated understanding
	Does not understand what is meant when asked to identify the need met by a specified kind of help.	Understands what is asked, but has difficulty identifying obvious needs met by very common kinds of help.	Identifies the obvious needs met by very common kinds of help.	Identifies the obvious needs met by many kinds of help.	Identifies the obvious and less obvious needs met by many kinds of help.

Comments:

Name(s):

Assess information retrieval

➤ Assess students' ability to extract information from books or interviews using the rubric *Assessing information retrieval* (Blackline Master #45). The source of evidence for extraction of book-based information is students' ability to answer the questions on *Our book research* (Blackline Master #41A–B); the source of evidence for extraction of interview information is students' ability to answer the questions on *Our Interview* (Blackline Master #42A–B). Reaching the "basic understanding" level on the rubric may be appropriate for many primary students who are new to the study of community.

Blackline Master #45

Assessing information retrieval

	Pre-recognition	Partial recognition	Basic understanding	Extended understanding	Sophisticated understanding
Extracting book-based information	Does not understand what it means to locate information in answer to questions using books that have been provided.	Understands the task, but has difficulty locating readily apparent book-based information in answer to simple questions.	Locates readily apparent book-based information in answer to simple questions.	Locates apparent book-based information in answer to questions.	Locates obvious and less obvious pieces of book-based information in answer to questions.
Extracting interview information	Does not understand what it means to locate information given orally in answer to specified questions.	Understands the task, but has difficulty locating readily apparent spoken information in answer to simple questions.	Locates readily apparent spoken information in answer to simple questions.	Locates apparent spoken information in answer to questions.	Locates obvious and less obvious pieces of spoken information in answer to questions.
Extracting non-verbal information	Does not understand what it means to locate non-verbal information in answer to specified questions.	Understands the task, but has difficulty locating readily apparent non-verbal information in answer to simple questions.	Locates readily apparent non-verbal information in answer to simple questions.	Locates apparent non-verbal information in answer to questions.	Locates obvious and less obvious pieces of non-verbal information in answer to questions.

Comments:

Name(s):

Assess important contributions

➤ Assess students' understanding of the importance of role contributions using the rubric *Assessing important contributions* (Blackline Master #46). The sources of evidence for this assessment are the starred contributions on the completed copy of *Our book research* (Blackline Master #41A–B) or *Our Interview* (Blackline Master #42A–B) and student responses on *Note of appreciation* (Blackline Master #43). Reaching the "basic understanding" level on the rubric may be appropriate for many primary students who are new to the study of community.

Assessing important contributions

Recognizes importance of role contributions	Pre-recognition Does not understand what it means to judge the importance of a role's contributions.	Partial recognition Understands what is asked, but has difficulty recognizing the importance of role contributions even in very obvious situations.	Basic understanding Recognizes the importance of role contributions in very obvious situations without providing any explanation.	Extended understanding Recognizes the importance of role contributions in obvious situations, offering very simple explanations of their importance.	Sophisticated understanding Recognizes the importance of role contributions in a range of situations, explaining in own words why they have the importance they do.
Comments:					

References

General

Bourgeois, Paulette. (1999). *Franklin's Neighbourhood* (illustrated by Brenda Clark). Toronto: Kids Can Press (ISBN 1-55074-704-5)

Caseley, Judith. (2002). *On The Town: A Community Adventure.* Harper Collins (ISBN 0-06-029584-8)

DiSalva-Ryan, DyAnne. (2001). *A Castle on Viola Street.* New York: Harper-Collins. (ISBN 0688176909)

Hassett, John & Hassett, Ann. (1998). *Cat Up a Tree.* Boston: Houghton Mifflin. (ISBN 0395884152)

Johnson, Dinah. (1999). *Sunday Week.* New York: Holt. (ISBN 0805049118)

Rockwell, Anne. (1987). *Come to Town.* New York: Crowell (ISBN 0690046448)

Community helpers

Animal hospital

Martin, C.L.G. (1994). *Down Dairy Farm Road.* New York: Macmillan. (ISBN 0027624501)

Bakers

Grossman, Patricia. (1991). *The Night Ones.* San Diego: Harcourt Brace. (ISBN 0152574387)

Bus drivers

Denslow, Sharon Phillips. (1993). *Bus Riders.* New York: Four Winds Press. (ISBN 0627286827)

Dentist

Berenstein, Stan & Jan. (1981). *The Berenstain Bears Visit the Dentist.* New York: Random House. (ISBN 0-39484-836-5)

Department store

Day, Alexandra. (1989). *Carl Goes Shopping.* New York: Farrar Straus Giroux. (ISBN 0374311102)

Firefighters

Bond, Felicia. (1984). *Poinsettia and the Firefighters.* New York: Crowell. (ISBN 0690044003)

Bourgeois, Paulette. (1992). *Canadian Firefighters.* Toronto: Kids Can Press. (ISBN 1-55074-042-3)

Munsch, Robert. (1983). *The Fire Station* (illustrated by Michael Martchenko). Toronto: Annick Press. (ISBN 1-55037-171-1)

Rey, Margaret. (1985). *Curious George at the Fire Station.* Boston: Houghton Mifflin. (ISBN 0-39539-037-0)

Garbage collectors

Bourgeois, Paulette. (1992). *Canadian Garbage Collectors.* Toronto: Kids Can Press. (ISBN 1-55074-040-7)

Gas station/ Garage mechanics

Aldag, Kurt. (1992). *Some Things Never Change.* New York: Macmillan (ISBN 0027002055)

McPhail, David. (1990). *Pig Pig Gets a Job.* New York: Dutton Children's Books. (ISBN 0525446192)

Grocery Store

DiSalva-Ryan, DyAnne. (2001). *Grandpa's Corner Store.* New York: Harper Collins. (ISNBN 6688167160)

Health care workers

Rey, Margaret. (1966). *Curious George Goes to the Hospital.* Boston: Houghton Mifflin. (ISBN 0-39507-062-7)

Berenstein, Stan & Jan. (1985). *The Berenstain Bears Go to the Doctor.* New York: Random House. (ISBN 0-39484-835-7)

Newspapers

Kunnas, Mauri & Kunnas, Tarja. (1985). *The Nighttime Book.* New York: Crown. (ISBN 051755819X)

Newspaper deliverers

Pilkey, Dave. (1997). *The Paperboy*. (Illustrated by Dave Pilkey) New York: Scholastic. (ISBN 0-590-10641-4)

Police officers

Bourgeois, Paulette. (1992). *Canadian Police Officers* (illustrated by Kim LaFave). Toronto: Kids Can Press. (ISBN 1-55074-133-0)

Rey, Margaret. (1987). *Curious George Visits a Police Station*. Boston: Houghton Mifflin. (ISBN 0-39545-349-6)

Postal workers

Bourgeois, Paulette. (1992). *Canadian Postal Workers*. Toronto: Kids Can Press. (ISBN 1-55074-058-X)

Restaurants

Lewin, Ted. (2002). *Big Jimmy's Kum Kau Chinese Take-out*. New York: Harper-Collins. (ISBN 0688160263)

Brandenberg, Alexa. (1997). *Chop, Simmer, Season*. San Diego: Harcourt (ISBN 0152009736)

Taxi drivers

Grover, Max. (1997). *Max's Wacky Taxi Day*. San Diego: Browndeer Press/Harcourt Brace. (ISBN 0152009892)

Teachers

Allard, Henry. (1997). *Miss Nelson Is Missing*. New York: Scholastic. (ISBN 0-590-11877-3)

Slate, Joseph. (1996). *Miss Bindergarten Gets Ready for Kindergarten* (Illustrated by Ashley Wolff). New York: E.P. Dutton. (ISBN 0-52545-446-2)

Thaler, Mike. (1977). *The Librarian from the Black Lagoon*. New York: Scholastic. (ISBN 0-679-89008-4)

Who am I?

Critical Challenge

**Critical
task**

Dramatize a community role found at your assigned community place for a game of charades.

Overview

In this challenge, students reinforce and expand their knowledge of community roles in the course of playing a game of charades. Students are assigned a place in the community and they must prepare a dramatization of a role found in that place. Among other criteria for an effective charade, students must indicate an important need met by their assigned role. Students practice their charade with team members and then perform them before the rest of the class who must guess the role.

Objectives

**Broad
understanding**

Many people contribute to meeting the needs of others in the community. Much information can be communicated with words.

**Requisite
tools**

Background knowledge
- knowledge of community roles and their contributions
- familiarity with game of charades

Criteria for judgment
- criteria for an effective role-play (e.g., informative, no words, simple, brief)

Critical thinking vocabulary

Thinking strategies

Habits of mind

Suggested Activities

Introduce charades

➤ Announce to the class that they are going to play charades. Determine whether or not all students are familiar with this game. If not, explain the premise of the game and the key rules (no sound, just actions). Present a simple dramatization of an action (e.g., driving in a car) and ask students to guess what you are doing. Explain to students that the theme of their game of charades will be community helpers/roles.

familiarity with game of charades

Develop common gestures

➤ Explain to students that the first step in dramatizing their role will be to let the audience know about an important need that their role helps the community to meet. This clue will help the audience narrow their guesses. Demonstrate a gesture or action for each community need. Possible examples are suggested below:

- food (hand to mouth gesture)
- health (flexing muscles)
- safety (grasping arms around self)
- learning (point to head)
- belong/feel loved (hands over heart)
- fun/happiness (hand gesture indicating smile)
- make a living (counting money)
- get around (riding a bicycle)

Practice these actions with the class and create a chart using simple stick drawings as a reminder.

Develop criteria for role-play

➤ As a class, agree on what makes an effective role-play. Refer to your role-play demonstration to illustrate relevant criteria. Possible criteria might be:

criteria for role-play

- shows an important need;
- makes clear actions;
- uses no words;
- shows information about the role;
- does not take long to act out.

Create teams and assign roles

➤ Organize students into teams of three. Every student is to prepare a charade. Students can involve team members in their charade, ask team members for ideas and practice their charade in front of them. Cut out and randomly distribute a community place card (Blackline Master #35A–D) to every student. Students are expected to prepare a role that is found at the community place indicated on their card (eg., library, hospital). If you anticipate that students will have difficulty with some roles, remove these place cards from the pile of cards to be distributed. Students should consult with their team members and with you if they do not know much about the place or about a role that might be found there. If necessary, give students new cards with more familiar roles. Remind students not to show their card to anyone except their team members.

Present the critical challenge

➤ When the teams are created and the community places are assigned, present the critical task:

Dramatize a role found at your assigned community place for a game of charades.

knowledge of role

Ask students to identify a role they would expect to find at their assigned community place and an important need met by this role. Encourage students to examine pictures on the map and other sources for information about their role.

Develop and practice role-plays

➤ Alone or with the assistance of team members, allow students time to develop a dramatization of their assigned role. Provide time for students to practice and refine their role-play with their team.

Play charades

➤ Before beginning the game, remind students of the following rules:

- The role must be shown in actions only. Voices cannot be used.

- Members of each team will act out their role-plays for everyone else to guess (not team members).

- The goal is to portray the role so well that others can guess its identity. (If you choose to award points, give each team one point when the class guesses its role.)

- Using one of the actions posted on the chart, start each charade by indicating the important need met by the role.

Rotate among the teams, so that one member from every team has an opportunity to perform before approaching a second member from any team.

Debrief the activity

➤ After everyone has presented a charade (or if the class is tired of the game for the moment), discuss what was effective and what was not. Distribute a copy of *Thinking about my learning* (Blackline Master #22) to each student. Read the questions together and ask students to think about their role-play and respond to the questions on the sheet. Ask students to draw a picture of themselves performing their role.

Evaluation   *Blackline Masters #45, 47*

Assess information retrieval

➤ Assess students' ability to extract information from non-verbal communication using the rubric *Assessing information retrieval* (Blackline Master #45). The source of evidence is students' ability to interpret the clues offered in the charades game. Reaching the "basic understanding" level on the rubric may be appropriate for many primary students.

Assess non-verbal communication

➤ Assess students' ability to communicate non-verbally using the rubric *Assessing non-verbal communication* (Blackline Master #47). The source of evidence is students' ability to dramatize clues about their role in the charades game. Reaching the "basic understanding" level on the rubric may be appropriate for many primary students.

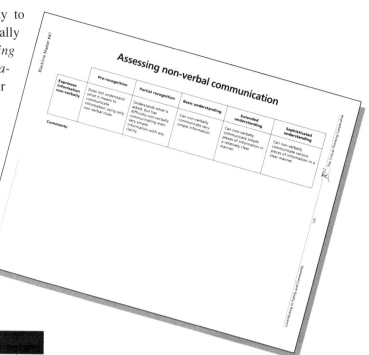

Extension

Play it again

➤ If students enjoyed and learned from the charades, redistribute the cards and hold another round of charades. Offer one or two pieces of advice about communicating ideas non-verbally that everyone might practice in this second round.

A three-star community?

Critical Challenge

Critical task

Decide whether we are a "three-star," "two-star" or "one-star" community.

Overview

In this final challenge, students bring closure to their exploration of the ways in which community members help to meet each other's needs. Students assemble evidence of community contributions accumulated throughout the unit in preparation for a "report card" or assessment of their community. Students study the evidence amassed on a giant wall chart, including evidence that community needs may not always be met. Students are introduced to three levels of "community stardom" and assign a rating to their community. As an extension, students create a certificate of merit for their community.

Objectives

Broad understanding

Many people in the students' community help in meeting the needs of its members.

Requisite tools

Background knowledge
- knowledge of contributions in the community

Criteria for judgment
- criteria for a great community (e.g., almost everyone helps to meet basic needs)

Critical thinking vocabulary
- evidence

Thinking strategies
- information chart

Habits of mind

Suggested Activities

Build a giant report card

➤ As a culminating activity for students' exploration of community contributions, we propose a class assessment of their community. We suggest that the "evidence" be assembled as a giant "report card" posted on the classroom wall. This chart would enable students to see a visual record of the information, largely already developed throughout the unit, about community members' efforts to meet each other's basic needs. The giant chart might take the form of the chart outlined below. The large scale of the wall chart is designed to encourage student accumulation of a lot of information and to dramatically represent the volume of contributions made by community members. (However, evidence of unmet needs may stimulate interesting discussion and serve as a catalyst for a community improvement project.) This challenge can be done on a smaller scale by not transferring the information that students record on *Meeting basic needs* (Blackline Master #39A–B) to the wall chart.

clue and conclusion

➤ Suggest several sample conclusions and invite students to offer clues that might lead to these conclusions:

Sample wall chart

Are people in _____ helping to meet everyone's needs?

	YES	MAYBE	NO
food			
health			
safety			
learning			
belonging/feel loved			
fun/happy			
make a living			
get around			

Session One   *Blackline Master #39*

Discuss evidence of greatness

➤ Begin by asking students if their community is a "good" place to live. Ask students for reasons for their opinion. As a way of prompting further discussion, ask if the community is a "great" community. Encourage students to convince you that it might be "great." Suggest that it is not sufficient simply to say "It's great," students need evidence to back up their conclusion. Explain that "evidence" is

evidence

information that people can offer as the reason why they think something is true and why others should also think it is true. Invite students to consider the following request for evidence:

- If I wanted to convince you that I did see a particular movie on television last night, what evidence could I offer? (describe the details of the movie, ask a family member to confirm, show the television schedule);

- If I wanted to show you that someone is a good friend, what evidence could I offer? (show you things they have given me, tell you what they do for me, ask them to tell you, send you to others to say that it is true).

- If I wanted you to believe that it is raining outside, what evidence could I offer? (take you outside, show you my wet clothes, show you the weather report).

Invite the class to suggest a few pieces of evidence to "prove" to you that the community is a great one.

Explore criteria for a great community ➤ Suggest to students that it would be easier to find evidence about the greatness of the community if all of us agreed on what a great community looked like. Prompt students' thinking about relevant criteria by discreetly suggesting each of the basic needs identified in this unit (see Blackline Master #39A–B for a list). You might ask, for example, "In a great community, would people feel like they belonged?" "Would everyone have the food they needed to eat?" "What about fun? Would people in a great community have fun?" At an appropriate point, suggest that a great community would be one in which people were working to ensure that everyone's needs were met. Now ask students for evidence of how people in their community are working to meet each other's needs. If students need help getting started, remind them of the information they gathered about community roles (e.g., grocers provide vegetables to meet people's food and health needs, doctors help people stay healthy, taxi and bus drivers help us meet our need to get around).

criteria for a great community

Introduce evidence gathering ➤ Once students get the idea of what would count as evidence, suggest that they keep a record of this information. Distribute an enlarged copy (11 x 17) of *Meeting basic needs* (Blackline Master #39A–B) to each pair of students. Review each of the needs on these two sheets. Explain that students are to look for as many pieces of evidence as they can to show that their community is working to meet these needs. Students should record a piece of information in each box underneath the need(s) to which it applies. Discuss with students how they might find this evidence:

information chart

- remembering what they have already learned;

- looking over their drawings and completed activity sheets;

- looking at books and local newspapers;

- talking to people;

- looking around the community.

Discuss whether each pair of students should complete both sheets together or whether each partner should initially focus on a different sheet (either Blackline Master #39A or #39B) and then switch sheets later on.

Discuss negative evidence

➤ At some point, students may notice that their community is not meeting everyone's needs. This revelation may be desirable as some balance in their perspective is healthy. If it does arise, suggest that students record evidence of unmet needs in a different colour than evidence of met needs. If students seem oblivious to unmet needs in their community, consider inviting students to look for evidence of needs that are not met. On the other hand, it may be more important to concentrate on building student pride in their community.

Sessions Two & Three

Introduce the community report card

➤ Soon after introducing the project, put up the large wall chart described earlier. Explain that soon (perhaps the next day or the day after that), students will place their evidence on this giant report card. In the interim, regularly ask students to share evidence orally with the rest of the class. Suggest that students use the following format:

- state a piece of information;

- indicate where the information came from ("I just remember" is fine);

- indicate which need is being met (or not being met).

Reinforce needs

➤ Allow students time to discuss with their partner and to look for additional evidence in books and other resources. Encourage students to find evidence for all eight needs. Duplicate extra copies of Blackline Master #39A–B in case students require additional sheets. If students are stuck for ideas, locate copies of the scenarios examined in Critical Challenge #4, especially the ones involving the mining town (Blackline Master #27), the small island (Blackline Master #29) and the big city (Blackline Master #31). Read the accompanying text, and ask students which of the services provided in these communities are also provided in their community. Then help students recognize the need(s) served by these contributions.

Session Four

Transfer evidence to chart

➤ When each pair of students has accumulated a large amount of evidence (or is tired of looking for evidence), invite students to transfer their information to the wall chart. There are several ways in which this can be done:

- the easiest method: Students simply cut out the strips of evidence for each need and paste the strips in the appropriate spaces on the wall chart.

knowledge of community contributions

- less easy method: Two pairs of students consolidate their collective evidence to reduce duplication. They neatly print their final list in large letters on cards or slips of paper which are then attached to the wall chart.

- more challenging method: Students cut out the strips of evidence for each need and hand over each strip to the team responsible for consolidating all the evidence for a particular need. In this option, teams of three or four students would examine all the evidence for a different need. The teams would neatly print their final selection in large letters on cards or slips of paper which are then attached to the wall chart.

Information that was designated (colour-coded) as evidence of unmet needs would be placed under the "no" column. Students may decide that some information may indicate that needs are met for some, but not for others. They may decide to place this kind of evidence in the "maybe" column. It is anticipated the bulk of the evidence will be in the "yes" column.

Discuss assembled evidence

➤ Once students' evidence is assembled on the wall chart, examine the findings:

- Invite students to comment on their first impressions or overall reactions to the assembled evidence.

- Discuss the (anticipated) lack of evidence of unmet needs. You might observe, for example, that although doctors work to keep us healthy, perhaps not all people have a doctor whenever they need one.

- Raise the (anticipated) relative lack of evidence for some needs. For example, if there is less evidence for "belonging," does this mean that the community does not do as good a job meeting this need as it does other needs.

- Ask students to share their most interesting or surprising piece of evidence.

If students show interest in gathering more evidence about particular matters, delay the overall rating of the community until this evidence has been complied.

Introduce the "star" scale

➤ After the class has discussed the issues raised by the evidence assembled on the wall chart, introduce the idea of deciding how great their community actually is. Begin by asking students if they know what it means to call someone a movie star or rock star. Draw out that these people are recognized as "really good" performers. Explain that although it is obvious that members of this community are stars, it is unclear how great they are. Suggest that there can be three levels of "community stardom." Display an overhead transparency of *Levels of community stardom* (Blackline Master #48) and review each level. Invite students to suggest a possible example of evidence for each level. Invite students to discuss their thoughts with a partner or in small groups.

Present the critical challenge

➤ After students have had an opportunity to think about the issue, present the critical task:

Decide whether we are a "three-star," "two-star" or "one-star" community.

Distribute a copy of *Starring our community* (Blackline Master #49) to each student (or pair of students). Ask students to record their rating and reasons on this sheet. Encourage students to use the evidence to decide which "star" rating their community deserves and to give good reasons for their star rating. Draw attention to the other questions on the sheet.

Draw closure

➤ After completing Blackline Master #49, invite students to read aloud their decisions and reasons to the class. Ensure that students who may have assigned a less popular "star" rating are not made to feel uncomfortable with their position. Encourage a feeling of celebration for the collective efforts both of the community in helping to meet its members' needs and of the class in learning about the many ways that people contribute to their community and family.

Evaluation
Blackline Masters #34, 50

Assess evidence charts

➤ Assess students' ability to provide evidence about the community contributions in meeting each need using the first criterion found on the rubric *Assessing understanding of community* (Blackline Master #34). Use students' responses recorded on *Meeting basic needs* (Blackline Master #39A–B) to assess their ability to support conclusions with information. Reaching the "basic understanding" level on the rubric may be appropriate for many primary students who are new to the study of community.

Assess the assessment

➤ Assess students' assessment of their "star" community as recorded on *Starring our community* (Blackline Master #49) using the rubric *Assessing the as-sessment* (Blackline Master #50). Reaching the "basic understanding" level on the rubric may be appropriate for many primary students who are new to the study of community.

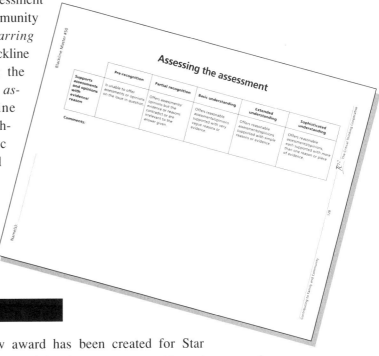

Extension

Design community award

➤ Explain that a new award has been created for Star Communities. This award is given to communities where people work together to meet each other's needs. Ask students to work with a partner to design a Star Community Award for their community. Display a variety of certificates and trophies as examples. Invite a member of the local municipal council to visit your classroom and receive the student-presented awards. Prepare for the visit by helping students develop questions that focus the council's role and efforts in meeting community needs.

Undertake community action

➤ If students have noticed where people's needs are not completely met, invite them to consider how they might help in this regard. A resource in this series, *I Can Make a Difference*, offers ten critical challenges for primary students on various aspects of family and community action, including solving interpersonal problems, helping an elderly person, preparing a package for a homeless person and aiding a stray animal.

References

Ford, Carole *et al.* (2003). *I Can Make a Difference.* Richmond: The Critical Thinking Cooperative and Ministry of Education, British Columbia. (ISBN 0-86491-262-5)

List of Blackline Masters

Our neighbourhood

People	Places

Things	Activities

67

What I would miss the most

Special people

1. _____

2. _____

3. _____

If I had to move, the person I would miss the most is _____

_____

because _____

_____

_____

Special places

1. _____

2. _____

3. _____

If I had to move, the place I would miss the most is _____

_____

because _____

_____

_____

Special things

1. _____

2. _____

3. _____

If I had to move, the thing I would miss the most is _____

_____

because _____

_____

_____

Special activities

1. _____

2. _____

3. _____

If I had to move, the activity I would miss the most is _____

_____

because _____

_____

_____

People: _____

Place: _____

Thing: _____

Activity: _____

TC^2 The Critical Thinking Cooperative

Assessing community features

	Pre-recognition	Partial recognition	Basic understanding	Extended understanding	Sophisticated understanding
Identifies different features of a community	Does not understand what is meant when asked to identify the people, places, things and activities in student's own community or in pictures of communities.	Understands what is asked, but has difficulty identifying even the most obvious people, places, things and activities in student's own community or in pictures of communities.	Identifies a few of the most obvious people, places, things and activities in student's own community or in pictures of communities.	Identifies the obvious people, places, things and activities in student's own community or in pictures of communities.	Identifies a wide range of people, places, things and activities in student's own community or in pictures of communities.
Selects memorable or important features	Unable to select any memorable or important features of the community.	Selects features of the community that are not very memorable or important.	Selects important but predictable features of the community without providing any explanation.	Selects important features of the community, offering simple explanations of their importance.	Selects important features of the community, explaining their importance in own words.

Comments:

Sample activities

Your neighbour's lawn is getting long. She has been sick and cannot cut it. You cut the lawn for her so she can relax and get better.

Marcie loves hockey. Whenever she goes to the ice rink, she dreams of becoming a famous hockey player.

You just bought a new bike so you can have a better chance of winning the race.

Jatinder loves riding horses. Jatinder's neighbour, Mrs. Lee, lets him ride her horse and, in return, Jatinder cleans out the horse's stall.

Activity cards

People gave money, clothes and food to the Brown family because they lost everything in a fire.	Everyone in town gave money to build a new sports arena.
I really like watching television when I do my homework or when I read a book.	My class tried to make sure that all new students felt safe and happy during their first week of school.
On Saturday my family meets at the local park for a baseball game.	I saved my money for weeks to buy a new toy.
Students offered a free babysitting service so parents could enjoy the school fair.	The roses in our garden were enjoyed all summer by everyone who walked by them.

Is it a contribution?

Contribution – YES	Contribution – NO
Reason: _____ _____	Reason: _____ _____
Reason: _____ _____	Reason: _____ _____
Reason: _____ _____	Reason: _____ _____
Reason: _____ _____	Reason: _____ _____
Reason: _____ _____	Reason: _____ _____

Making a contribution

Activity	What kind of benefit? (What needs are met?)	How many people benefit?	How long do people benefit?	This action contributes...
I am a doctor. Every day I help sick people get better.				☐ a lot ☐ some ☐ a little because:
Every year on Earth Day, our class plants a tree in the park.				☐ a lot ☐ some ☐ a little because:
I drive a bus for the people who live in a nursing home.				☐ a lot ☐ some ☐ a little because:
I was the buddy for a new person in our class on her first day.				☐ a lot ☐ some ☐ a little because:

Making a contribution

Activity	What kind of benefit? (What needs are met?)	How many people benefit?	How long do people benefit?	This action contributes...
I helped a boy who could not find his way to the store.				☐ a lot ☐ some ☐ a little because:
The choir I sing in performs every week at the seniors' home.				☐ a lot ☐ some ☐ a little because:
I watch my little sister when my mom makes dinner.				☐ a lot ☐ some ☐ a little because:
I am a police officer. Every day I help keep people safe.				☐ a lot ☐ some ☐ a little because:

$\mathcal{TC}^2$ The Critical Thinking Cooperative

Assessing community contributions

	Pre-recognition	Partial recognition	Basic understanding	Extended understanding	Sophisticated understanding
Determines whether or not actions are contributions	Does not understand what it means to decide whether an action makes a contribution to others.	Understands what is asked, but cannot consistently distinguish of actions that contribute to others that do not, without providing any explanation.	Correctly distinguishes very obvious examples of actions that contribute to others from those that do not, without providing any explanation.	Correctly distinguishes obvious examples of actions that contribute to others from those that do not, offering a very simple explanation.	Correctly distinguishes even in less obvious situations, actions that contribute to others from those that do not, explaining the reason in own words.
Assesses the significance of contributions	Does not understand what it means to assess the significance of contributions to others.	Understands what is asked but has difficulty in assessing the significance of contributions to others even in very obvious situations.	Can assess in the most obvious situations the significance of contributions to others, without providing any explanation.	Can assess in obvious situations the significance of contributions to others, offering very simple explanations.	Can assess in a range of situations the significance of contributions to others, explaining the reasons in own words.

Comments:

Picture #1

77

 The Critical Thinking Cooperative

Picture #2

Picture # _____

Studying pictures

	Clues	Conclusions
What *is the person doing?*		
Where *is this? (What is the place?)*		
Who *is the person?*		
Why *is the person doing it? (What need is the person meeting?)*		

Picture #3

TC^2 The Critical Thinking Cooperative

Picture #4

ST REMY L 3138
FINE FRENCH BRANDY

Picture #5

TC² The Critical Thinking Cooperative

Picture #6

The Critical Thinking Cooperative

Picture #7

Picture #8

85

TC^2 The Critical Thinking Cooperative

Picture #9

Picture #10

The Critical Thinking Cooperative

Assessing picture studies

	Pre-recognition	Partial recognition	Basic understanding	Extended understanding	Sophisticated understanding
Distinguishes clues from conclusions	Does not understand the difference between a clue and a conclusion.	Understands the difference, but cannot consistently distinguish obvious examples of clues from conclusions.	Correctly distinguishes very obvious examples of clues and conclusions, without providing any explanation.	Correctly distinguishes obvious examples of clues and conclusions, offering a very simple explanation.	Correctly distinguishes many examples of clues and conclusions, explaining the connection in own words.
Recognizes clues and draws conclusions	Does not understand what it means to locate clues in order to reach a conclusion.	Understands what is asked, but has difficulty locating clues and using them to reach a very obvious conclusions.	Locates the most obvious clues to reach a single obvious conclusion.	Locates obvious clues to reach one or more conclusions.	Locates a range of obvious and less obvious clues to reach multiple conclusions.

Comments:

The Brown family

The Brown family lives in an apartment on First Street. Mrs. Brown goes to work to earn money so that she can pay rent for a place to live. Then she can also buy clothes, food, medicine, books, tools and other things her family needs for school and for play. The neighbour looks after the two children after school until Mrs. Brown gets home from work. The children help by feeding the dog, keeping their rooms tidy and drying the dishes. On holidays, Mrs. Brown and her two children play games, tell each other stories, and go to the beach, the library, the museum and to baseball and soccer games at the park. The family also likes to swim at the city pool on the weekend. Sometimes the Brown family has a BBQ with their friends.

TC² The Critical Thinking Cooperative

Thinking about my learning

One thing that was hard for me in this activity was _____

_____

One thing that was easy for me in this activity was _____

_____

I learned   ❑ about myself
              ❑ about others
              ❑ about communities

One thing I learned is _____

_____

People at the beach

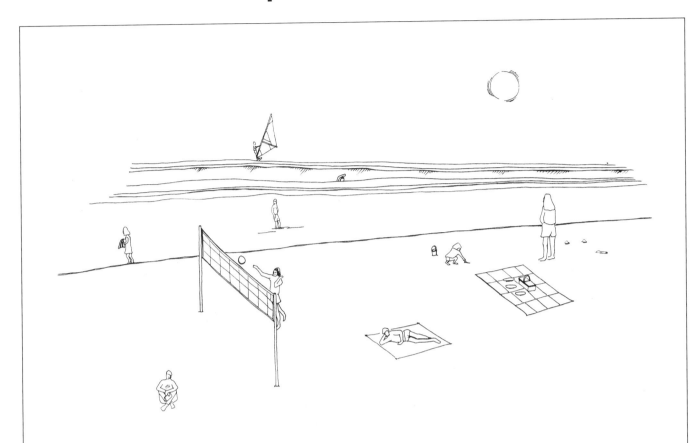

People went to the beach to enjoy the sun, the sand and the water. They did not talk with each other. Each person sunbathed, swam and had a good time. Some ate food they brought from home. Some stayed in the sun too long and got sunburns. Then each person packed up and went home.

TC² The Critical Thinking Cooperative

What we see and hear

Name of the people: _____

People (who)	Places (where)	Things (what they have)	Activities (what they do)

					People (who)	Places (where)	Things (what they have)	Activities (what they do)

Picture: _____

Is this a community?

Is everyone interacting? (Are people working and playing with each other?)

YES	MAYBE	NO

Is everyone interacting? (Are people working and playing with each other?)

YES	MAYBE	NO

The _____

☐ is
☐ is not
☐ may be

a community

because _____

A hermit

The hermit lives alone in the shelter he made from the trees and brush where he lived. He hunted and fished for his food and got clean water from the brook nearby. He made his own clothes from the things he found in nature. The plants, water and animals around him provide all of the company he wants.

People in a mining town

People who live in this mining town have places to live in town and at the iron mine. They buy food, clothes, tools and toys at the general store. They buy fresh bread at the bakery. There is lots of clean water to drink. There are also three restaurants where people can buy meals. People can buy fresh vegetables when the ship comes to town. A water taxi carries people to small villages nearby. Airplanes that land on the water bring the mail to people and people also travel on them. A man in town delivers oil when people need it for cooking and for heating their homes.

Some people work up the hill at the iron mine, some go logging at nearby logging camps, some go fishing and some work in town. There is an elementary school for children. A priest or a minister comes to town on Sundays for people who wish to go to church. The doctor comes to town once a week so that people who are sick can visit her. There is a volunteer fire department to help put fires out. The RCMP come to town on Saturday nights in case people need help.

For fun, some people hike in the woods or go boating and fishing. Because this is a small town, most people know each other. There is a community hall where movies are shown on Saturday night. Sometimes there are dances, school plays, town meetings and other special events.

People at a mountain resort

People love to gather at the mountain resort. In the winter, there are lots of things to do—downhill skiing, cross-country skiing, tobogganing and snowshoeing. Some people skate on the nearby lake. Other people like to gather in front of the big stone fireplace and share stories with each other. In the summer, you can go hiking, swim at the lake, play tennis at the court, or spend the day in the sun by the pool.

The restaurant serves good food. Or people may bring their own food to cook in the small kitchens in their rooms. A doctor lives at the resort in case anyone gets sick or hurt. There is also police and fire protection. The roads are kept open all year in case there is an emergency.

Some people who do not have to go back to work to earn money, live here all year round. Other people work at the resort and do not have to leave it at all. There are enough stores to provide everything that people need.

People living on a small island

People move to the small island because they want a peaceful life. There are places to live and there are carpenters to build houses or to fix them. The store sells food, milk, pop, juice, vegetables, newspapers and even ice cream! It also sells lottery tickets. The store also has a small coffee shop where you can buy soup, sandwiches and drinks. One store sells books, art supplies and crafts. There is also a small hardware store and another small store sells food and videos. The bakery sells yummy pizza and soup, coffee and fresh bread. Some farms sell fresh fruit and veggies during the summer.

There is an elementary school for island children, a volunteer fire department and even a doctor. If people get sick and need a hospital, they go by ferry or helicopter to a hospital on Vancouver Island. For fun, people go hiking, biking, boating and fishing. There is a community centre for special events and town meetings.

Families at the beach

Families often head for the beach for the summer. Once there, it is hard to leave. There is lots of room for swimming and a life-guard, who is on watch all day. There are food stands everywhere with fish and chips, hot dogs, veggie wraps, sandwiches, ice cream, pop, coffee, fruit drinks and milk. Or families can make their own meals in the cottages they rent for the summer. Some stores sell clothes, tools and food. Other stores rent boats and fishing supplies. People set up tents on the beach to sell crafts.

Some people live at the beach all year. These are people who do not have to work or people who work near the beach to provide all of the things the summer visitors want. Families who visit the beach may not know each other but after a few days they might begin to talk and do things together.

People living in a big city

Some people like to live in a big city. They like the many things you can find in a city—fancy restaurants, hamburger restaurants and many kinds of stores to buy clothing, shoes, food, pets, music and books, toys, sporting goods, cars and household goods. There are small schools and big schools, churches, universities, art galleries, museums, recreation centres, sports stadiums, and different kinds of entertainment at the many theatres. There are libraries, parks and swimming pools, as well as police and firefighters in almost every neighbourhood. There are big hospitals and lots of doctors if anyone gets sick.

There are all sorts of places for people to live—apartments, townhouses, trailers, houses and sometimes even boat houses, mansions and castles. There is TV in almost every home. If parents want to go out, babysitters are available to look after the children. There are lots of ways to travel—by bike, bus, car, truck, train, plane and boat.

TC² The Critical Thinking Cooperative

The O'Hara family

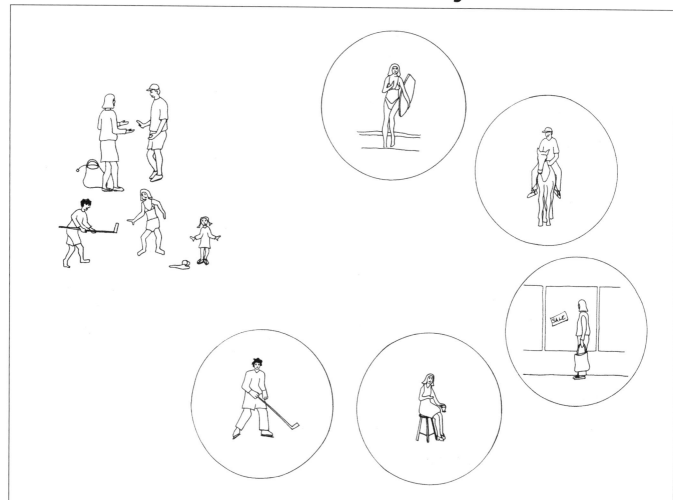

There are five people in the O'Hara family, but they never see each other anymore. The three children have grown up and moved away and the parents have not heard from them for many years. The parents do not live together anymore. They are much happier living far apart in different parts of the province.

People in a school

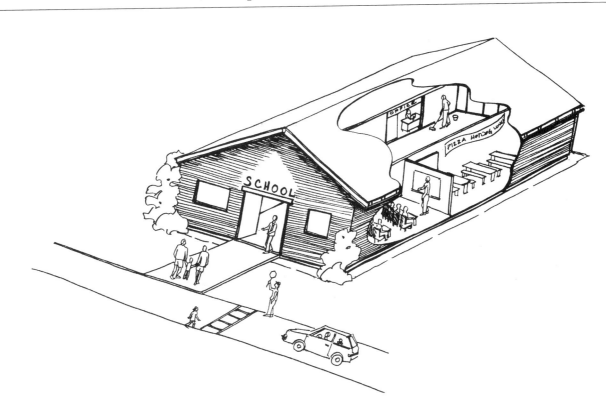

Lots of people work in schools: some to learn, some to teach and others who help in different ways. The principal looks after everyone, making sure that children are learning and that teachers have what they need to teach. Parents often come to school to see how their children are doing and to find out how they can help. Sometimes, parents come to school to make hotdogs and order pizzas for everyone for lunch. Some parents help plan special events where people have fun and raise money for field trips or to buy new equipment for the school. The secretary looks after things in the office. The custodian keeps the school tidy and clean.

Teachers help students learn. Students come to school to learn to be successful citizens. At school, students make friends and have time to play games. Special teachers help students learn as well. Teachers sometimes have assistants who help in the classroom. Some people help at school cross walks so students do not get hit by cars. Some people cut the lawns so students have a place to play.

Assessing understanding of community

	Pre-recognition	Partial recognition	Basic understanding	Extended understanding	Sophisticated understanding
Supports conclusions with information	Does not understand what is meant when asked to provide information to support differing conclusions.	Understands what is asked, but has difficulty providing relevant information to support even very obvious conclusions.	Provides only the most generally obvious pieces of information to support conclusions.	Provides several obvious pieces of information to support conclusions.	Provides a range of obvious and less obvious pieces of information to support conclusions.
Decides whether a group is a community	Does not understand what it means to decide whether or not groups of people are communities.	Understands what is asked, but has difficulty deciding whether or not groups of people are communities even in very obvious situations.	Decides in the most obvious situations whether or not groups of people are communities, but cannot explain why they cannot meet the identified criteria.	Decides in obvious situations whether or not groups of people are communities, offering very simple explanations why they meet the identified criteria.	Decides in a range of situations whether or not groups of people are communities, explaining in own words why they meet the identified criteria.

Comments:

Community places

animal hospital	bakery
barber shop	restaurant
video store	garage
church	grocery store
bank	post office
fire hall	newspaper

gas station	community hall
arena	soccer field
hospital	police station
radio station	library
dental clinic	home
doctor's office	swimming pool

golf course	bowling alley
market	park
flower shop	nursery
landfill	drug store
movie theatre	TV station
radio station	school

court house	bus station
taxi stand	city hall
department store	hair salon
art gallery	day care
seniors' residence	building supply store
recycling depot	security company

Help cards

I had a toothache.	I wanted a haircut.
I wanted to find out about dinosaurs.	I wanted to see a funny movie.
I needed to get my noisy car fixed.	I had a flat tire.
I wanted a loaf of bread.	I wanted something to eat right away.
I needed a new pair of boots.	I had to mail a parcel to my grandma.
I had a sore ear.	I fell and hurt my arm.
I needed to get medicine for my cat.	I found a stray dog.

I needed to get rid of very big pieces of garbage.	I wanted to return a lost wallet to its owner.
I wanted to listen to the news.	I wanted to sell my bike.
I wanted to get to the skating rink.	I wanted to play with my friends.
I saw an accident on my street.	I needed to find a home for my grandma because she can't live alone anymore.
I wanted to plant a garden.	I wanted to take a karate class.
I wanted to learn more about photography.	I needed to buy milk.
I wanted to get rid of empty bottles.	I wanted to have a stop sign put on my street.
I wanted to learn to read and write.	

My own community adventure

I woke up one morning and _____ *needed help*

so I decided to go to _____ *community place*

when I got there I met _____ *roles*

and then _____ *how they helped*

1. _____

I just got home when _____

I ran to _____

Once inside I saw _____

I was so happy _____

2.

A little later _____

3.

I don't know why but _____

4.

And finally _____

Assessing community places and roles

	Pre-recognition	Partial recognition	Basic understanding	Extended understanding	Sophisticated understanding
Knowledge of community places, roles and services	Does not understand what is meant when asked to identify the roles and services associated with identified places in the community.	Understands what is asked, but has difficulty identifying an obvious role and service associated with the most common places in the community.	Identifies an obvious role and service associated with the most common places in the community.	Identifies an obvious role and service associated with many places in the community.	Identifies more than one role and service associated with common and less common places in the community.

Comments:

Meeting basic needs

food	health	safety	learning

				belong/feel loved
				fun
				make a living
				get around

I am curious about...

Places or roles I want to find out about...	I would like to know...

I am curious about...

Places or roles I want to find out about...	I would like to know...

Our book research

I found information about my role in _____

written by _____

Q. What is the community role or job you are researching?	A.

Q. Where do people in this role work?	A.

Q. What things or equipment are found at this place?	A.

How does this role help people in the community meet their needs?

Q. Does the role help people LEARN?	A.

Q.	A.
Does the role help people be SAFE?	
Q.	A.
Does the role help people be HEALTHY?	
Q.	A.
Does the role help people have FUN?	
Q.	A.
Does the role help people BELONG?	
Q.	A.
Does the role help people GET AROUND?	

Q.	A.
_____ _____ _____	

Our interview

Hello, _____

Our names are _____
Thank you for agreeing to answer our questions.

Q. What is your role or job in our community?	A.

Q. Where do you work?	A.

We have been studying how people in our community help meet each other's needs.

Q. In your role, do you help people LEARN?	A.

Q.	A.
In your role, do you help people be SAFE?	
Q.	A.
In your role, do you help people be HEALTHY?	
Q.	A.
In your role, do you help people have FUN?	
Q.	A.
In your role, do you help people BELONG?	
Q.	A.
In your role, do you help people GET AROUND?	
Q. _____ _____ _____	A.

Thank you for answering our questions.

TC^2 The Critical Thinking Cooperative

Note of appreciation

To: _____

Role: _____

Place: _____

We appreciate many things that you do to help our community meet its needs:

1. _____

2. _____

3. _____

But we REALLY appreciate how you help the community meet its need to

_____

when you _____

Thank you very, very much.
Signed _____

Assessing understanding of needs

	Pre-recognition	Partial recognition	Basic understanding	Extended understanding	Sophisticated understanding
Knowledge of ways needs are met	Does not understand what is meant when asked to identify the need met by a specified kind of help.	Understands what is asked, but has difficulty identifying obvious needs met by very common kinds of help.	Identifies the obvious needs met by very common kinds of help.	Identifies the obvious needs met by many kinds of help.	Identifies the obvious and less obvious needs met by many kinds of help.

Comments:

Assessing information retrieval

	Pre-recognition	Partial recognition	Basic understanding	Extended understanding	Sophisticated understanding
Extracting book-based information	Does not understand what it means to locate information in answer to questions using books that have been provided.	Understands the task, but has difficulty locating readily apparent book-based information in answer to simple questions.	Locates readily apparent book-based information in answer to questions.	Locates apparent book-based information in answer to questions.	Locates obvious and less obvious pieces of book-based information in answer to questions.
Extracting interview information	Does not understand what it means to locate information given orally in answer to specified questions.	Understands the task, but has difficulty locating readily apparent spoken information in answer to simple questions.	Locates readily apparent spoken information in answer to simple questions.	Locates apparent spoken information in answer to questions.	Locates obvious and less obvious pieces of spoken information in answer to questions.
Extracting non-verbal information	Does not understand what it means to locate non-verbal information in answer to specified questions.	Understands the task, but has difficulty locating readily apparent non-verbal information in answer to simple questions.	Locates readily apparent non-verbal information in answer to simple questions.	Locates apparent non-verbal information in answer to questions.	Locates obvious and less obvious pieces of non-verbal information in answer to questions.

Comments:

TC^2 The Critical Thinking Cooperative

Assessing important contributions

	Pre-recognition	Partial recognition	Basic understanding	Extended understanding	Sophisticated understanding
Recognizes importance of role contributions	Does not understand what it means to judge the importance of a role's contributions.	Understands what is asked, but has difficulty recognizing the importance of role contributions even in very obvious situations.	Recognizes the importance of role contributions in very obvious situations without providing any explanation.	Recognizes the importance of role contributions in obvious situations, offering very simple explanations of their importance.	Recognizes the importance of role contributions in a range of situations, explaining in own words why they have the importance they do.

Comments:

Assessing non-verbal communication

	Pre-recognition	Partial recognition	Basic understanding	Extended understanding	Sophisticated understanding
Expresses information non-verbally	Does not understand what it means to communicate information using only non-verbal clues.	Understands what is asked, but has difficulty non-verbally communicating even very simple information with any clarity.	Can non-verbally communicate very simple information.	Can non-verbally communicate simple pieces of information in a relatively clear manner.	Can non-verbally communicate various pieces of information in a clear manner.

Comments:

Levels of community stardom

★★★	★★	★
Your community deserves three stars if **almost everyone** in the community is helping to meet people's needs.	Your community deserves two stars if **most people** in the community are helping to meet people's needs.	Your community deserves one star if **some people** in the community are helping to meet people's needs.

Starring our community

★ ★ ★	★ ★	★
Your community deserves three stars if **almost everyone** in the community is helping to meet people's needs.	Your community deserves two stars if **most people** in the community are helping to meet people's needs.	Your community deserves one star if **some people** in the community are helping to meet people's needs.

I think our community deserves a rating of
- ❑ ★★★
- ❑ ★★
- ❑ ★

I think this because _____

_____

_____

The best thing about our community is _____

_____

_____

I think our community could improve if _____

_____

_____

One thing I could do to make our community even better is _____

_____

_____

Assessing the assessment

	Pre-recognition	Partial recognition	Basic understanding	Extended understanding	Sophisticated understanding
Supports assessments and opinions with evidence/ reason	Is unable to offer assessments or opinions on the issue in question.	Offers assessments/ opinions but the evidence or reasons contradict or are irrelevant to the answer given.	Offers reasonable assessments/opinions supported with very vague reasons or evidence.	Offers reasonable assessments/opinions supported with simple reasons or evidence.	Offers reasonable assessments/opinions, each supported with more than one reason or piece of evidence.

Comments: